USING DIGITAL VIDEO IN INITIAL TEACHER EDUCATION

Critical Guides for Teacher Educators

You might also like the following titles from Critical Publishing.

Becoming a Teacher Education Researcher
Eds Diane Mayer and Ian Menter
ISBN: 9781913453299

Tackling Anxiety in Primary Mathematics Teachers
By Karen Wicks
ISBN: 9781913453015

The Teacher Educator's Handbook: A narrative approach to professional learning
By Elizabeth White with Miranda Timmermans
ISBN: 9781913453657

Understanding Feedback
By Caroline Elbra-Ramsay
ISBN: 9781913453251

Our titles are also available in a range of electronic formats. To order, or for details of our bulk discounts, please go to our website www.criticalpublishing.com or contact our distributor Ingram Publisher Services by telephoning 01752 202301 or emailing ipsuk.cservs@ingramcontent.com

USING DIGITAL VIDEO IN INITIAL TEACHER EDUCATION

Series Editor: Ian Menter

Critical Guides for Teacher Educators

John McCullagh

First published in 2021 by Critical Publishing Ltd

British Library Cataloguing in Publication Data
A CIP record for this book is available from the British Library

ISBN: 9781913453336

This book is also available in the following e-book formats:
EPUB: 9781913453350
Adobe e-book reader: 9781913453367

Cover and text design by Greensplash Limited
Project Management by Deanta Global Publishing Services, Dublin, Ireland
Typeset by Deanta Global Publishing Services, Chennai, India
Printed and bound in Great Britain by 4edge, Essex

Critical Publishing
3 Connaught Road
St Albans
AL3 5RX

www.criticalpublishing.com

Paper from responsible sources

CONTENTS

	About the series editor and author	*vi*
	Foreword	*vii*
Chapter 1	How can video support learning in initial teacher education?	1
Chapter 2	The role of video in microteaching	12
Chapter 3	Using video to support classroom observation	24
Chapter 4	From passive to active learning: Interacting with video	35
Chapter 5	Using digital video to develop reflective practice	48
Chapter 6	Video and the assessment of classroom practice	63
Chapter 7	Theoretical perspectives on the value of using video in ITE	72
	References	*83*
	Index	*95*

ABOUT THE SERIES EDITOR

Ian Menter is former President of BERA, 2013–2015. At Oxford University Department of Education he was Director of Professional Programmes and led the development of the Oxford Education Deanery. Before moving to Oxford, Ian was Professor of Teacher Education at the University of Glasgow. Prior to that he held posts at the University of the West of Scotland (Dean of Education and Media), London Metropolitan University (Head of School of Education), University of the West of England and the University of Gloucestershire. Ian was President of the Scottish Educational Research Association from 2005 to 2007 and chaired the Research and Development Committee of the Universities' Council for the Education of Teachers from 2008 to 2011. He is a Fellow of the Academy of Social Sciences and a Fellow of the Royal Society of Arts and is a Visiting Professor at Bath Spa University and Ulster University and an Honorary Professor at the University of Exeter. Since 2018 he has been a Senior Research Associate at Kazan Federal University, Russia.

ABOUT THE AUTHOR

John McCullagh is a senior lecturer in science education at Stranmillis University College where he teaches on the primary and post-primary education programmes and contributes to the College's professional development courses for teachers. His research interests include the use of collaborative approaches to initial teacher education such as coteaching and the use of digital video. He is a Fellow of the Royal Society of Chemistry and involved in science curriculum development in primary science and chemistry. Before working in higher education he taught science at secondary level in Northern Ireland.

FOREWORD

Learning to teach is a complex and challenging process. In a 12-nation comparative study of teacher education systems carried out with Maria Teresa Tatto, I was able to identify six cross-cutting themes that could be used to indicate the condition of each of those systems. The sixth theme, and the one that I suggested was most speculative, was that of digitization (Menter, 2019). I suggested:

it seems that while student teachers are being encouraged to make use of IT [Information Technology] in their classrooms and in preparing to teach lessons, the adoption of electronic forms of learning for the students themselves has not been developing rapidly.

(Menter, 2019, p 276)

It is in the light of this observation that it is a great delight to be publishing John McCullagh's book, which so carefully sets out a constructive approach to the use of video in the processes of learning to teach. Over the course of several years, he has been researching and developing the use of these technologies with a view to ensuring high-quality and productive learning for pre-service teachers. In this text he is able to demonstrate the theoretical strengths of his approach as well as providing very practical guidance to those readers who seek to adopt similar methods in their own contexts.

While demonstrating the powerful learning insights that can be gained from the use of video, he also pays careful attention to the ethical and affective dimensions of the processes and procedures that he has adopted.

It has become all too apparent during the pandemic of 2020–2021 that technology-based learning of all kinds has been a lifeline for the continuation of schooling (Breslin, 2021). This is no less true in teacher education, where not only video itself but also remote meeting platforms – where video films can be aired – have been crucial in maintaining the preparation of new teachers to be ready to enter the profession.

This is therefore a great addition to our series, and John is to be congratulated for his commitment and for his scholarship, as so well represented in this book.

Ian Menter
Series Editor, Critical Guides for Teacher Educators
Emeritus Professor of Teacher Education, University of Oxford

References

Breslin, T (2021) *Lessons from Lockdown.* London: Routledge.

Menter, I (2019) The Interaction of Global and National Influences, in M T Tatto and I Menter (eds) *Knowledge, Policy and Practice in Teacher Education – A Cross-National Study.* London: Bloomsbury.

CHAPTER 1 | HOW CAN VIDEO SUPPORT LEARNING IN INITIAL TEACHER EDUCATION?

CRITICAL ISSUES

- *Why can video technology support the learning of pre-service teachers?*
- *How can video address some of the challenges of learning to teach?*
- *How should video-based activities be designed to maximise learning?*

Introduction

Digital video technology has much to offer initial teacher education (ITE), both through the technological affordances it brings to the study of teaching and from its potential to mediate the collective construction of knowledge. The powerful combination of moving images and sounds speaks to us more profoundly than any other form of media. They bring an immediacy and intimacy which draws on our capacity as humans to be moved, made curious and to reason. Video can prime us to feel involved in the action, to wonder about unfolding events, and, most importantly, it can inspire us to think and talk. Advances in digital technology and the proliferation of mobile devices allow pre-service teachers (PSTs) to meaningfully engage with practice, away from the ITE institution or school setting and at times and in places of their choice. It also provides teacher educators with the means to capture and present practice with its complexity unravelled, yet its detail and its authenticity preserved.

This introductory chapter considers the affordances of video and how it can be used to develop PSTs' understanding of teaching and develop their planning, teaching and evaluating skills. It explores how video may help teacher educators overcome the challenges presented by the complex nature of teaching and engage PSTs in meaningful, authentic learning tasks. Video, however, is only a tool for learning, and its use requires careful thought and planning. Therefore, the chapter also identifies factors which may limit the effectiveness of using video and explores the underlying principles which should underpin and guide how video-related activities should be designed.

The use of video within ITE

The facility to record, replay and analyse teachers' actions has remained the fundamental feature of using video within ITE. Sherin's (2004) historical overview describes how its aims have been shaped by teacher educators' notions of what is teaching and have shifted in line with the prevailing theoretical framework on learning. As the behaviourist view of teaching as the execution and sequencing of particular actions evolved from the late 1960s into a more cognitive model of learning in the 1980s, greater consideration was given to what teachers were *thinking* as well as how they were *behaving.* Therefore, the objectives of video use moved beyond mastering specific instructional techniques to developing PSTs' subject content knowledge and their understanding of the relationship between learning and teaching (Rich and Hannafin, 2009; Santagata et al, 2005). As video cameras became more accessible and easier to operate and the process of recording less obtrusive, the use of classroom footage grew in popularity. The increase in the quality of recordings and the ease with which they could be made now allowed for the objectification of practice and provided individuals with the means to evaluate and reflect on their teaching. Advances in digital technology and internet connectivity provide novices and experienced teachers alike access to a wider and more diverse range of teaching approaches and enable the sharing of new and alternative forms of pedagogy within and across learning communities. In this twenty-first century, Feiman-Nemser (2001) points out that reform-minded teaching, which adopts a learner-centred problem-solving approach, further shifts conceptions of teaching as *telling* and learning as *listening*, to teaching as the *eliciting* of pupils' ideas and learning as the *construction* of conceptual understanding. This form of teaching requires a more focused and nuanced approach to the interactive aspects of practice and requires teachers who are skilled in responding to the moment-by-moment needs of learners and whose thinking is both reflexive and reflective. As digital video has been shown to be an invaluable tool for the continuing professional development of in-service teachers (Baecher, 2020; Marsh and Mitchell, 2014; Martin and Siry, 2012), its use within ITE will equip PSTs with the skills and disposition to continue to explore and extend their practice throughout their teaching careers and so blur the boundary between the pre- and in-service phases of teacher education.

How can video help PSTs learn about teaching?

The videos used in ITE can help structure PSTs' introduction to the classroom, serve as exemplars of the proficient practice of a particular teaching skill or provide them with the opportunity to observe and evaluate their own first attempts at being a teacher. The recordings can feature either the PSTs themselves or others (Figure 1.1).

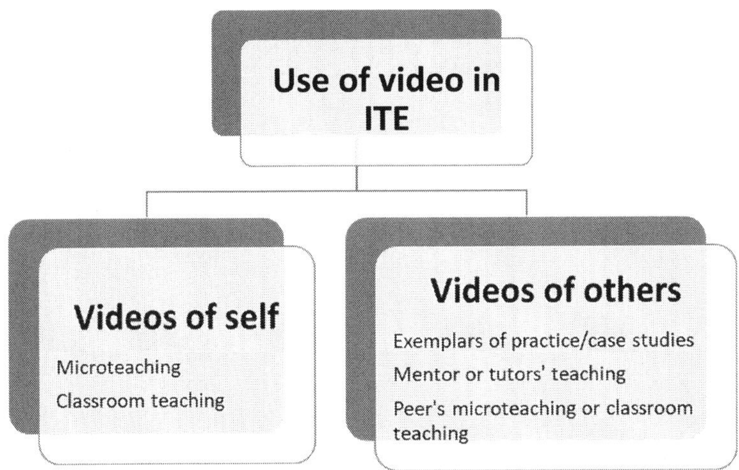

Figure 1.1 Videos can feature either the PST themselves or a teacher or peer

A number of researchers (Abell and Cennamo, 2004; Brophy, 2004; Goldman et al, 2007) have proposed that video helps PSTs to *activate* their beliefs and thinking about teaching and learning, helps them *acquire* competence and knowledge and enables them to *apply* them within a meaningful setting (Figure 1.2).

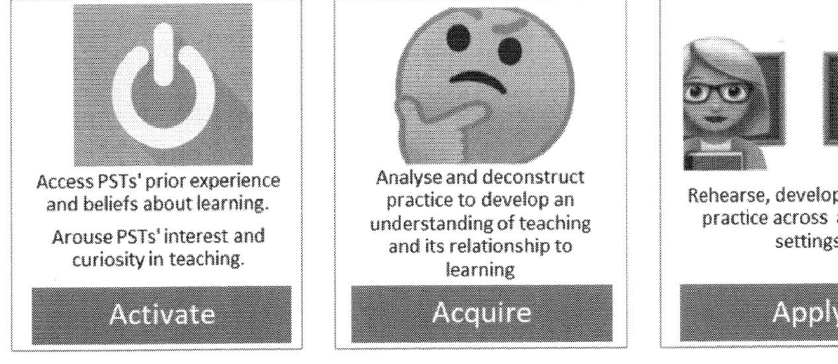

Figure 1.2 How videos can help support PSTs in learning to teach

Reflection

» What activities do you use to encourage PSTs to discuss their own experience of schooling? How do you respond to their feedback?

Activate

Unlike the case in other professions, PSTs bring to their studies experiences and beliefs about teaching acquired during their own schooling. This 'apprenticeship of observation' (Lortie, 1975) has been shown to influence how PSTs think about teaching (Luft, 2001) and can be resistant to change (Luehmann, 2007). It is, therefore, important that from the very outset of their training, PSTs have the opportunity to discuss their own learning experiences and explore their existing beliefs, particularly where they may be at odds with the forms of pedagogy exemplified during the ITE programme (Bachivan and Cobern, 2016). There is also a view that acknowledging these prior experiences may identify and affirm effective forms of practice and teacher behaviours (Mewborn and Tyminski, 2006).

Videos can also extend PSTs' exposure to classroom scenarios beyond their personal experience and challenge their assumptions and thinking (Yadav and Koehler, 2007). Recordings of typical classroom scenarios can be used by teacher educators to prompt memories and elicit perceptions, and, crucially, help create the supportive environment best suited for exploratory discussion (Goodman, 1988). The real and vivid nature of classroom images and sounds can engage learners and help '*create the mental context that prepares them to learn, … bring to bear relevant knowledge*, and … *make sense of subsequent instruction*' (Schwartz and Hartman, 2007, p 339). Video recordings can also be used to draw attention to the positive impact which good practice can have on pupil progress and thus inspire and motivate PSTs. Feiman-Nemser (2001, p 1017) believes that PSTs '*must also form visions of what is possible and desirable in teaching*'.

Acquire

Video recordings can conveniently transport PSTs to a range of classrooms where they can see and hear for themselves many examples of different teaching–learning scenarios. As a result, they come to witness what Marsh and Mitchell (2014, p 405) describe as

complex sets of circumstances which may be resistant to verbal representation and which in any event may be more clearly and powerfully demonstrated by 'real people in real situations' than be by the abstraction of a teacher educator at one remove from the classroom activity.

The facility to pause, replay and re-watch enables the learner to break down parts of the lesson into more learnable 'chunks' (Le Fevre, 2004). The use of shorter clips ensures that '*the often antagonistic goals of presenting complexity and making learning cognitively manageable are simultaneously achieved*' (Spiro et al, 2007, p 97). Controlling the detail and the pace with which the lesson is presented to the learner ensures that a fine-grain analysis of practice is possible without losing any sense of the overall meaning of the lesson.

Apply

Recordings of lessons can provide a real context in which PSTs can begin to plan, evaluate or offer critiques and alternative approaches to teachers' behaviours, in line with authentic scenarios. Their understanding can be road tested away from the demands of an actual classroom and with the support of tutors and peers. This proxy form of knowledge application can allow for tasks to be infused throughout all stages and levels of learner proficiency within an ITE programme and so ensure challenge and progression.

Video and skills development

A number of studies have identified how video can help PSTs become proficient in particular skills such as planning and evaluating (McCullagh et al, 2013), managing the classroom (Weber et al, 2018) and engaging pupils in the learning process (Gibbons and Farleys, 2019). Video has also been reported to enhance learners' overall understanding of classroom practice (Lofthouse and Birmingham, 2010) and their ability to reflect critically on their practice (McFadden et al, 2014; Harford and MacRuairc, 2008; Rosaen et al, 2008; Rickard et al, 2009). Stroupe and Gotwals (2018) have used video to help PSTs attempt more challenging forms of science teaching they call 'approximate ambitious instruction'. The facility to look closely and repeatedly at specific teacher actions and behaviours within an authentic and complete teaching episode highlights how individual incidents contribute to the bigger picture of the overall lesson.

Reflection

» How do you help PSTs to understand the relationship between teaching and learning?

The challenging nature of learning how to teach

Digital video can be used to help address three fundamental challenges which PSTs confront when learning how to teach. Firstly, teaching may seem easy and straightforward, with the craft, wisdom and skill of the teacher remaining invisible to the untrained idea. The often-tacit and multi-faceted nature of the teacher's knowledge and skill can make it difficult for PSTs to see and appreciate what they should be attending to during their observation of a lesson. Secondly, teaching is highly complex, described by Spiro et al. (2007, p 93) as an ill-structured domain, '*in which the instances of knowledge application are both individually complex and in irregular relationship to each other*'. Teaching scenarios develop from minute to minute and vary widely across settings, and so it is not possible for the teacher to have a '*pre-packaged prescription*' (Spiro et al 2007, p 93) of what to think or how to act in all circumstances. Teacher educators are therefore tasked with deconstructing practice and presenting it in an accessible form.

Finally, there is the issue that the practice element of the ITE programme usually takes place in a different setting away from the support of tutors and peers and often occurs asynchronous to the study of related theory. Any differences in the priorities, resources and educational culture of both learning sites and the limited opportunity for collaboration and discussion may restrict PSTs' opportunities to connect theory to practice, explore alternative teaching approaches and make for a less-than-gentle and supportive induction into the profession. As placement may well be the learner's first encounter with pupils, it is the point at which they need the most support, guidance and reassurance. Grossman and McDonald (2008, p 189) raise the question of why '*university-based teacher educators leave the development of pedagogical skill in the interactive aspects of teaching almost entirely to field experiences, the component of professional education over which we have the least control*'. They also point out that tasks requiring PSTs to begin to apply their knowledge and understanding are usually limited to planning or evaluating, with actual interactive teaching rarely included. Therefore, ITE programmes should provide opportunities for learners to attempt interactive teaching within the controlled scenarios of reduced complexity.

Reflections

» How do you first introduce classroom teaching to PSTs at the beginning of ITE?

» What informs and guides your approach?

Using video to introduce and develop practice

Video-supported learning activities can help overcome the challenges identified earlier regarding the development of PSTs' understanding and enactment of practice. Grossman et al's (2009) study of training programmes for professional practices related to '*human improvement*' (p 2057), such as teaching, clergy and clinical psychology, have identified three key concepts for understanding the pedagogies of practice in professional education: *representations, deconstructions* and *approximations of practice*. Representations of practice refer to activities which make practice explicit and learners more mindful of its elements. Deconstruction of practice breaks it down into smaller units of action and thought, while approximations of practice covers activities which take place away from the professional setting. Table 1.1 shows examples of activities relating to each concept and their benefits.

Table 1.1 Examples and benefits of video-based activities for Grossman's (2009) three pedagogies of practice

Video-supported activity	Benefits to PSTs
Representations of practice scaffolded by • Viewing and discussing exemplar lessons. • Viewing videos from a diverse range of classrooms and teaching scenarios. • Viewing videos representing case studies. • Recording videos of personal practice for inclusion in e-portfolios.	• Presents detail and allows for tutor commentary and explanation. • Extends PSTs' experience and enables them to identify patterns and establish key principles of practice. • Facilitates a problem-based approach to learning. • Enables PSTs to see and evidence their attainment and recognise progression in their practice, thereby nurturing professional agency.
Deconstruction of practice assisted through • Pausing of video at key moments in the lesson. • Slowing down or replaying parts of the video recording. • PSTs annotating the video with comments or responses to prompts or questions. • Video editing tasks to identify and select specific aspects of practice.	• Allows for the lesson to be broken down and analysed through open discussion. Observation skills can be extended by freezing the frame and sharing interpretations. • The detailed nature of fast-moving events is revealed, and PSTs become attuned to what they may have failed to notice. • Transforms the role of PST from passive viewer to active learner. Annotations and responses enable tutors to access and challenge PST thinking. • Editing requires close viewing of the same clip several times and draws closer attention to pupil or teacher behaviours.
Approximation of practice enacted during • Microteaching. • Video recording of pairs or small teams of PSTs teaching lessons to small groups of pupils. • Drafting lesson plans based on their viewing of video recordings of lessons. • Creating and sharing evidence-based evaluations of video recordings of lessons.	• Provides PSTs with their first experiences of planning, teaching and evaluating in a controlled and supportive setting. • Allows for the transfer and consolidation of learning from microteaching into a more authentic and challenging situation. Video analysis can identify improvement in practice from microteaching and thus provide reassurance and develop confidence. This further develops agency and vindicates reflection as a tool for development. • Video recordings of lessons provide the framework around which PSTs can create written accounts of practice and develop the ability to envisage how written lesson plans might look like in the classroom and how intended practice may be accurately represented in lesson plans. • Develops PSTs awareness of what and where to look for regarding evaluation. Collaboration with peers and tutors requires assertions to be evidence-based.

Reflection

» What issues have restricted your use of video?

Attending to the limitations of video

While video can serve as a considerable aid to PSTs, it is worth considering the factors which could potentially limit its value and how they may be overcome. Erickson (2007) points out that viewers are accustomed to watching a video which has been carefully edited and designed to infer meaning, and less used to watching longer clips of unedited footage. What is shown in the video is limited to the particular camera angle and focus, and so the viewer is not able to make decisions about where to look and what to attend to as the lesson unfolds. It is this limitation which prompted Gardner and McNally (1995) to contend that video could be no substitute for the live classroom experience. The viewer is also not party to any conversations or events off-camera which the recording may miss, yet which may have guided the teacher's decisions and actions. With this in mind, Fadde and Zhou (2015) observe that teachers' own stand-alone recordings can be less useful than professionally edited recordings despite being more 'natural'. However, acknowledging and discussing this '*video conundrum*' (p 201) with PSTs can cause them to engage more critically with video-based classroom analysis and pay closer attention to how they might make their own recordings. The use of two cameras to record the lesson from different angles, for example from both the front and back of the classroom, allows the viewer to see the lesson from the perspective of both teacher and pupils. Some video playback software such as iMovie allows for split-screen presentation, providing the viewer with the unique opportunity to see how pupils react (or not!) to the actions of the teacher and how the teacher responds. (Muting the audio playback on one recording avoids the need for synchronising both recording devices.)

The content of edited video is controlled by what the editor considered to be important and may exclude classroom footage which others may have found useful or interesting. It can also be difficult to acquire a sense of the duration of the various parts of the lesson. Providing additional information about the context of the lesson, such as how the lesson fits into the topic or scheme of work, the ability range of pupils or the teacher's expectations for the lesson (Shwartz and Hartman, 2007) helps the learner to connect and compare the specific events they see and hear in the recording to wider issues and principles of education. Valuable additions to video recordings can include the following.

» *Hyperlinks* – These may be inserted into the video, linking to texts which provide background information to the lesson, lesson plans, worksheets, etc.

- *On-screen prompts or questions* – Annotations can be added on-screen or tagged by time markers to a text box below the screen. Spiro et al (2007, p 95) go as far as using sound effects booming, '*it's not that simple, look again*!' at particular parts of the video which are then re-played to draw viewers' attention and encourage them to reappraise the situation. They take the view that '*habits of mind are hard to change. Video affords ways to catch people's eye and to call attention to the often unconscious assumptions they are making*' (p 95).
- *Commentary* – The tutor can record a narration (for example, an explanation of what is happening in the video, how it relates to theory, alternative teacher actions), or the teacher featured in the video could share their perspective on the lesson (aims, objectives, previous or follow-up lessons, evaluation). This can provide an otherwise-missing insight into the teacher's thinking (Richardson and Kyle, 1999). Teacher evaluation could also be added as a separate audio or video file.

Planning video-based activities

Video is, however, only a tool for learning (van Es et al, 2015), and the overall benefit to PSTs depends on how activities are planned and facilitated (Tekkumru-Kisa and Stein, 2017). Most studies of the use of video in teacher education have focussed on the outcomes for teachers and PSTs, with only limited research into the pedagogy of its use (Blomberg et al, 2014). Blomberg et al (2013) identify five key principles which should guide the planning of video-based learning activities. Planning should identify a clear learning goal or goals and adopt an instructional approach in line with the desired outcome. In designing the activity, instructors should carefully consider their choice of video content and consider what additional material may be useful to learners. They recommend that the form of assessment should enable the learner to clearly demonstrate their attainment of the particular learning objective. Table 1.2 suggests how each of Blomberg et al's (2013) principles could be addressed when designing activities.

A similar framework for designing tasks is proposed by Tekkumru-Kisa and Stein (2017), who also pay particular attention to the role of the facilitator before and during the activity. By anticipating any events in the video which may be a source of surprise or disagreement, the facilitator can contemplate how best to manage and direct the discourse. Facilitators should also closely monitor group discussions and respond where appropriate to clarify, redirect, counter or validate opinions and use PSTs' comments to progress thinking and build understanding.

Table 1.2 Examples of how each of Blomberg's (2013) principles for guiding the use of video might inform the choice and design of related tasks

Considerations for designing a video activity	**Examples**
Identify learning goals	• Access and explore PSTs' perceptions of 'good' teaching. • Develop particular skills, for example planning, evaluating, asking questions, providing feedback, introducing lessons, managing transitions within or between lessons, organising group work, managing resources. • Develop PSTs' awareness of strengths and areas of development in their practice. • Develop PSTs' ability to reflect on and modify their practice. • Develop PSTs' subject knowledge and subject pedagogical content knowledge via video clips of the teaching of progressively more difficult concepts within a topic.
Align instructional approach to learning goal(s)	• Instructional approach can adopt either a cognitive (scaffolded and structured) or situated (detailed and open-ended) approach to learning. • The design may challenge PSTs to engage individually or in groups, with the task of observation, teaching or reflecting.
Acknowledge and mitigate against limits of video	• Challenge PSTs to declare 'what other information would be useful to know about this situation?' • Provide contextual information orally, on the screen or as additional documents. • Invite PSTs to suggest which additional footage or camera shots would be worth viewing.
Choose appropriate video content	• Exemplar videos are useful for characterising best practices. A range of settings allow general principles of theory to emerge. • Unedited videos of the lesson allow for a more nuanced critique, provide wider scope for discussion and can draw PSTs to question assumptions or challenge aspects of the practice. • Footage of self and peers can provide affirmation and reassurance and so enhance confidence.
Base assessment on evidence of goal attainment	• Assessment task could require editing and annotating a video. • Video of personal teaching alongside reflective annotations or written evaluations could evidence attainment of competences.

IN A **NUTSHELL**

Digital video can serve as an invaluable learning aid to PSTs because video recordings can present and preserve the full detail of the classroom and digital technology can facilitate rich learning activities. It can capture practice, provide a means for its analysis and empower learners to evaluate their progress. However, instructors must understand how to ensure that PSTs' attention is drawn to relevant information and that they are supported in their construction of new knowledge and not distracted or overwhelmed. To maximise learning, video-based activities should adopt appropriate instructional designs, select suitable video content and employ meaningful assessment methods in line with clear learning objectives.

REFLECTIONS ON **CRITICAL ISSUES**

- *Video technology can help PSTs' learning by providing authentic examples of teaching which they can discuss and analyse alongside guidance from tutors and in-service teachers. Digital technology enables classroom footage to be viewed alongside supporting text, which can direct the learner's attention and provide context further insight.*
- *Learning to teach is difficult as the skill and knowledge behind a teacher's classroom practice require exposition and structured explanation. Video technology allows for this to take place in and away from the classroom. The realness of video recordings can stimulate the discussion of teaching between PSTs and tutors and cause them to reflect on their own notions and pre-conceptions about learning.*
- *Video is a useful tool, but the efficacy of related tasks depends on the careful consideration of the learning goals, the role of the instructor and the use of appropriate video recordings and supporting artefacts.*

CHAPTER 2 | THE ROLE OF VIDEO IN MICROTEACHING

CRITICAL ISSUES

- *What is microteaching, and what are its reported benefits?*
- *How does video support learning within microteaching?*
- *How should video-related tasks be arranged to maximise learning?*

Introduction

Microteaching is generally used in ITE programmes to ease PSTs into the challenge of classroom teaching. It typically involves video recording PSTs as they teach a short lesson to their peers within an ITE institution. The recording is then used to support peer feedback and self-evaluation. The activity was first devised in the 1960s at Stanford University and then quickly spread to Europe. Klinzing and Floden (1991) provide a thorough account of its early history and development. The popularity of microteaching in the UK grew in the 1970s from a dissatisfaction with current methods of initial teacher education, particularly the separation of practice from theory and the arbitrary and unstructured opportunities for classroom observation and practice (McIntyre et al, 1977). Developments in video and digital technology and the shift to more collaborative and practice-related forms of teacher education have sustained its popularity within ITE programmes. This chapter discusses the aims and purpose of microteaching and examines the role of video in supporting learning.

What is microteaching?

Although used within initial teacher preparation programmes across the world, an exact definition of microteaching is hard to find. A good starting point might be the description provided by Dwight Allen, the then Associate Professor of Education at Stanford University (1967, p 1), where the activity was first developed.

The technique allows teachers to apply clearly defined teaching skills to carefully prepared lessons in a planned series of five to ten-minute encounters with a small group of real students, often with an opportunity to observe the results on videotape. Its distinction lies in the opportunity it provides teachers for immediate and individual diagnostic evaluation of teacher performance by colleagues, supervisors and participating students and for measuring progress in specific teaching techniques.

The key features identified in Allen's description (reduced lesson duration, use of video and the provision of feedback) have all featured in the design and evaluation of almost all studies of microteaching to date. Although the particular design and procedures of microteaching have varied over time, the aim of reducing the complexity of the classroom is common to many descriptions.

- *'Scaled-down teaching encounter in which pre-service teachers demonstrate their ability to perform one of several desirable teacher abilities to a group of three to five peers during a short time period'* (Cruickshank and Metcalf, 1993, p 87).
- *'The opportunity to practice in an instructional setting in which the normal complexities are limited'* (Benton-Kupper, 2001, p 830).
- *'Teaching for a short period of time normally focussing on one particular aspect of a lesson or teaching technique'* (Morrison 2010, p 19).

These descriptions highlight microteaching's objective of reducing the challenge of teaching for the first time. Whilst the word 'micro' may be taken to refer to a shorter lesson duration involving a small teaching group, it could also suggest very close observation or detailed analysis, as in 'putting teaching under the microscope'.

The benefits of microteaching

Microteaching has been the subject of numerous studies and reports. The reported benefits include the progression of teaching skills, development of reflective and critical thinking and the enhancement of confidence and self-efficacy beliefs, as shown in Table 2.1 below.

The aims and outcomes of microteaching have evolved over time in line with changes in the conceptualisation of initial teacher education, particularly the shift from a view of teaching as a definitive set of technical skills and abilities to a wider understanding of the multidimensional facets of practice. Schön's (1983) notion of reflective practice rejected a technical rational model of teaching as applied theory and gave rise to the notion of the teacher as a reflective practitioner engaged in a problematic enterprise through which skills, knowledge and ability are developed over time through reflecting on experience (Korthagen et al, 2001). This resulted in a wider view of microteaching as more than just an activity to develop teaching technique. A key study which challenged Zeichner's (1983)

Table 2.1 The reported benefits of microteaching

Reported benefits for pre-service teachers	**Reference**
Better planning skills	Bell (2007)
Enhanced instructional methods	Roth et al (2006)
Exploration of cause–effect dynamics of their actions	L'Anson et al (2003)
Better lesson evaluation skills	Napoles (2008)
Better presentation and communication skills	Benton-Kupper (2001)
Connection of theory to practice	Fernandez (2010)
Develop reflective thinking skills	Amobi (2005)
Critical thinking skills	Arsal (2015)
Increased pedagogical content knowledge (PCK)	Bahcivan (2017)
Enhanced self-efficacy beliefs	D'Alessio (2018)
Increased confidence and motivation	Subramaniam (2006)
Reduced anxiety	Peker (2009)

dismissal of microteaching as a narrow technical exercise compared the relative benefits of on-campus microteaching to in-school placements (Metcalf et al, 1996). It was found that PSTs who had been exposed to a series of microteaching activities were able to reflect on their teaching and experiences at a higher level than student teachers who had been placed in actual classrooms. Microteaching PSTs were claimed to have become *'more attuned to specific details of pedagogical situations'* and *'better able to transfer learning into new contexts'* (p 280). As the goals of microteaching moved beyond merely the acquisition of presentational skills and became more focussed on connecting teaching and learning, the term 'microteaching laboratories' ceased to be used to describe its setting. Microteaching activities, no longer restricted to purpose-made recording rooms, became integrated into more authentic teaching settings such as seminar rooms or actual classrooms (Metcalf et al, 1996; Benton-Kupper, 2001).

How does video support learning within microteaching?

Evidence of the impact of microteaching on the practice of pre-service teachers has been gathered from a number of studies adopting a range of methodologies. A popular approach has been to compare scores or ratings based on researchers' judgements of candidate's competence or teaching performance before and after one or more cycles of microteaching (Van der Westhuizen and Golightly, 2015). Comparisons have also been made between control groups and groups who have experienced microteaching (Arsal, 2015). Alternatively, a number of studies (Zhang and Cheng, 2011; Yalmanci and Aydin, 2014; Akalin, 2005) have focussed on direct feedback from pre-service teachers regarding their experiences of microteaching and explored if and how they valued it as a learning activity. Exploring PSTs' experiences of microteaching may inform and guide the development of future procedures and protocols.

The following case studies emerged from the 'Video in STEM Teacher Assessment' (VISTA Project) (McCullagh and Murphy, 2015) funded by the Standing Committee for Teacher Education North and South (SCoTENS). The project explored if pre-service teachers found microteaching useful and then sought a consensus on what they considered to be its key features. Case Study 1 reports on the views of participants from an ITE institution in Northern Ireland on the completion of two cycles of microteaching. Case Study 2 extended the number and nature of participants by including pre-service teachers from a different institution in the south of Ireland. By searching for consensus from pre-service teachers from two different ITE programmes, it was hoped that the findings would be more significant and therefore make the recommendations more transferable to other ITE settings.

Case Study 1

This case study involved 16 PSTs in the first year of a BEd degree programme in secondary science education. The first microteaching activity required the students to work in teams of two or three to plan, teach and evaluate a short science lesson to the rest of the group and their tutors. Each PST was required to teach for six minutes, and the topic was chosen by the tutor from the Key Stage 3 science curriculum. The lesson topic was decided by the group and they each taught a discrete aspect of the lesson, for example the introduction, a short pupil practical activity or the plenary. The lesson was video recorded by the tutor and made available to each group after the session. Each group was required to meet in their own time, view the recording of their lesson and identify what they considered to be strengths and areas for development in their teaching. Each group presented their analysis, supported by video clips, at an evaluation seminar the following week, during which the whole group were invited to provide feedback on each group's teaching and discuss each other's evaluations. During the seminar, the course tutor suggested strategies for addressing some of the areas for development identified in the videos. Each student then received one-to-one tutor feedback on their teaching and suggestions for development.

In the second microteaching session, the PSTs took responsibility for selecting the topic for the lesson, recording, downloading and sharing the video file and designing the lesson observation prompt sheet used by their peers. The PSTs requested that the tutors did not attend the teaching session. The evaluation task required the PSTs to look for evidence of improvement in the areas identified during the previous session and highlight aspects of their teaching which they feel they could develop further. This time the PSTs were required to produce short edited video clips to support their assertions. The PSTs produced and presented their edited videos at an evaluation seminar during which peers and the course tutors provided feedback on their progress.

All participants produced a short written account of what they found useful about the two microteaching sessions. The most frequently cited advantage (cited by all but two of the PSTs) was observing a particular aspect of their practice in the video and having a clearer sense of how this could be improved. This was particularly helpful for planning and evaluating.

Planning: '*I could see what the contents of my lesson plan actually looked like in action and how I needed to keep the class interested.*'

The opportunity to directly observe what a lesson plan actually looked like when enacted enabled the PST to make a critique of its delivery and content and highlighted the importance of planning for pupil engagement.

Evaluating: '*I would never have realised I said "ok?" so often and how I was often turning my back on the class. I think I was speaking too quickly for "children" to follow as well.*'

Reviewing the video recording was reported to pick up otherwise-undetected imperfections, as well as allowing for judgements about the pace of teacher talk.

The most commonly cited themes related to the use of video are shown in Figure 2.1. As well as providing a real and detailed picture of practice, the experience of seeing themselves teaching may help ease the sometimes-challenging transition from PST to teacher, as one respondent put it '*I felt I was at times like a real teacher and convinced me that I could actually do this*'.

As well as supporting the cognitive challenges of learning to teach, microteaching also attended to PSTs' affective needs. The experience of watching and engaging in video-related tasks greatly enhanced the PSTs' confidence, motivation and resilience.

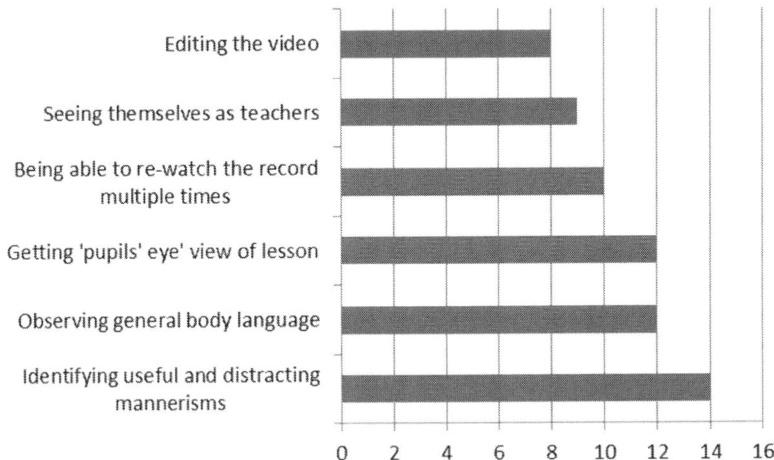

Figure 2.1 How frequently a video-related theme was cited as useful during microteaching (N = 16)

> *It was far less daunting when we were working in a group and it really eased us into classroom teaching. We were all in the same boat and wanted each other to do well. I also felt getting feedback from peers was easier as you knew them and trusted them and you could see it also from the video.*
>
> Simply 'seeing' themselves as teachers consolidated their commitment to the profession and enhanced their motivation and enthusiasm for development.

Maximising the learning from microteaching

A principal affordance of video identified in the feedback is the opportunity to see what has or hasn't happened during the short teaching episode. As well as providing the chance to notice the more obvious aspects of presentation, the video recording can now serve as a vital resource for comparing what *actually* happened to what was *intended* to happen. However, the extent to which this 'seeing' and reflecting result in professional growth is greatly influenced by how the video-related activities are designed and carried out. How should these tasks be designed to fully utilise the potential of the video recording?

In the second case study, we again sought direct feedback from PSTs regarding what features of two microteaching activities they had found to be useful.

Case Study 2

In this study the pre-service teachers from Case Study 1 collaborated with 14 postgraduate science education student teachers from the south of Ireland. Two microteaching sessions were held, one in each jurisdiction. For operational reasons the PSTs from the host institutions planned and resourced the microteaching lessons in advance of the microteaching session. The working groups included both sets of students, with the visiting students taking the lead during the evaluation task and the presentation of the group's edited video clips. At the PSTs' request, tutors were not present during the teaching sessions, with the responsibility for video recording resting solely on the PSTs themselves. The PSTs and tutors jointly agreed the programme for the second microteaching seminar, along with the lesson evaluation protocol and classroom observation template. A questionnaire was used to identify which features of the microteaching arrangements the students considered to enhance its effectiveness (N = 25). Focus group interviews allowed for fuller descriptions of their recommendations. The findings directly relating to the use of video are shown in Figure 2.2.

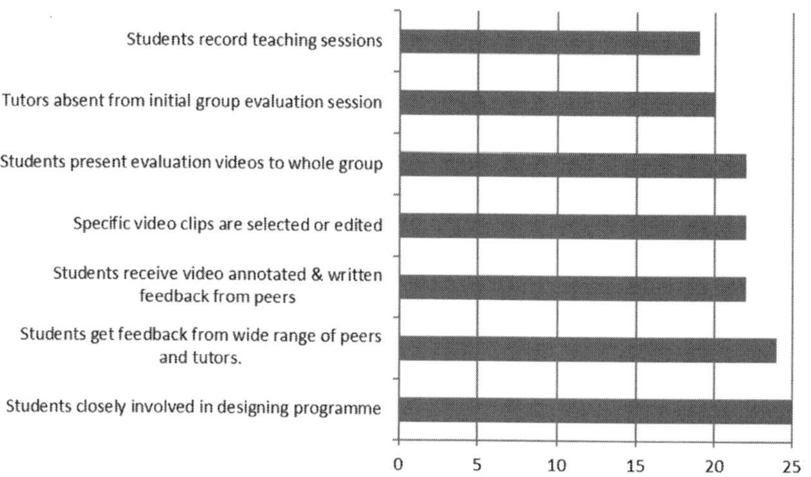

Figure 2.2 The number of PSTs who consider each of the listed features of microteaching to be an 'important' or 'very important' factor in determining its effectiveness (N = 25)

The feedback and comments indicate that microteaching is most effective (Figure 2.3) when it is:

» learner-centred – PSTs have control of the process of recording and analysing the video;

» collaborative – PSTs are required to plan and evaluate together;

» product-oriented – evaluation tasks generate a resource to support development.

How video is used within microteaching has a strong bearing on the extent to which these three prescriptions for effective microteaching are addressed. Table 2.2 suggests how video should be used to maximise learning.

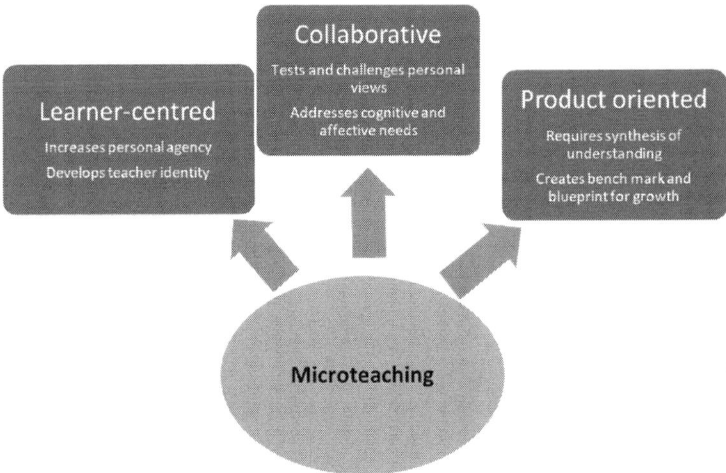

Figure 2.3 The video-related features of effective microteaching

Table 2.2 How video-related activity can support the key needs of learners

Feature	Role of digital video
Learner-centred	• Pre-service teachers take control of recording and decide on the positioning of the camera in line with the focus and learning objective of the microteaching. • Tutors are not present during the recording of microteaching sessions. • Pre-service teachers own their video recording and control its distribution.
Collaborative	• A shared understanding of the aims of the session is required between 'teacher' and recorder. • Video recordings are shared within and between groups and with tutors. • Peer and tutor feedback is based on video evidence and requires group consensus.
Product oriented	• Analysis of practice tasks involves selecting and editing video clips or adding time-marked annotations. • Personal and peer comments include suggestions for alternative approaches. • Lesson evaluation assignments take the form of an edited or annotated video.

Learner-centred

Prior to the digital age, the facility to record microteaching lessons resided only with tutors and therefore positioned PSTs as the objects of the activity. Today access to affordable high-definition cameras, smartphones or mobile devices puts PSTs directly in control of recording, sharing and analysing their own and their peer's teaching and so empowers them. The ability to microteach without the approval or involvement of a tutor and, at a time and place of their convenience, calls for greater agency on the part of the learner. This, in turn, could result in a shift towards what Brown and Duguid (1991) describe as 'demand-style' learning, where they have greater control over what they feel they need to learn, how they learn it and with whom they choose to collaborate. This calls for a dialogue between tutors and PSTs regarding which aspects of practice they wish to focus on and how the activities should be organised in order to achieve this. This move to more 'learner-centred microteaching' has been reported as beneficial by Kilic (2010), where students decide on the learning objectives of their microteaching sessions and help construct the lesson observation form. This increase in the meta-cognitive aspects of learning and greater independence could prove invaluable over the course of extended periods of school placement where contact with tutors or peers may be limited. Zeichner (1996) highlights the importance of ensuring that PSTs have the skills and the disposition to be pro-active with respect to their professional development. As PSTs gain experience and become more competent during their school placements, they develop their identity as teachers. Burn and Mutton (2015) point out the need for support in sustaining their identity as *learners*, as well as *teachers*, as it is only this which will ensure they continue to learn in new contexts and in the face of different challenges. Zeichner (1996, p 217) goes as far as describing ITE practices which do not nurture a capacity for continual professional growth as '*miseducative*'.

The potential for groups of PSTs to organise their own microteaching sessions independently from tutors also helps with the challenge of having many PSTs and so little time. Parallel microteaching sessions can be held, or groups could arrange to meet and microteach at a time which fits their timetable. Video recordings, with or without comments, can then be shared with tutors. PSTs requested that tutors were not present during the recording of lessons and suggested that it can be useful if they are also absent from some of the lesson evaluation group discussions. It was felt that this made for a more 'risk free' environment (Brent et al, 1996), where students are more likely to be honest and less defensive in the face of feedback and suggestions of alternative approaches (Amobi, 2005). Indeed, feedback is more honest and of greater value when it is not included within the assessment rubric within the ITE programme (Amobi, 2005; Brent et al, 1996; Kuswanodo, 2014).

Collaborative

The video recording of a microteaching lesson is a priceless resource enabling pre-service teachers to learn from both the *process* and the *product* of video analysis. In objectifying the practice, the video recording presents how they came across to the class and what *actually* happened in contrast to what the PST *hoped or believed* to have happened. Whilst the video recording can be used to produce a useful outcome (in the form of an edited or annotated video or a written evaluation), video facilitates close and meaningful collaboration and enables PSTs to learn from the process of evaluation. The viewing of their practice can remind and prompt the pre-service teacher to reflect on, 'What was I attempting to do here? Am I being effective?' and crucially, 'How might I improve this?' The views and opinions of peers are useful here as the PST attempts to rationalise or justify their actions. The resultant dialogue may explore the veracity of latent perspectives and tacit assumptions about teaching as well as pointing out things which may not have been noticed or considered unimportant. The collaboration also provides support and encouragement for the members of the group, promoting a collegial spirit and a sense of trust, which may help de-personalise the critique of the lesson by making it seem less about any shortcomings in the abilities of the *teacher* and more about how to improve a particular aspect of their *teaching*. Kuswandono (2014) proposes that a 'collectivist culture' is more likely to create the 'willingness' and 'seriousness' to engage in thinking again about teaching and views these requirements as crucial for effective microteaching. Siry and Martin (2014) describe how video-based 'co-generative dialogue' shifts the focus from individuals to the whole group and makes for a more powerful and transformative experience. The video recording and resultant dialogue provide both a means and a resource for reflection and '*promote noticing with an explicit focus on change*' (p 502). By identifying priorities, the edited or annotated video can serve as a blueprint for change and encourage a more forward-looking stance. It introduces the notion that whilst reflection is based on what has happened in the past, it should always be focussed on the future. Similarly, Digby (2017) reports that video-stimulated dialogue provides an effective form of professional development for practitioners in early-year settings. The video served as a prompt and a context for an exploration of the relationship between teachers' actions and pupil learning and allowed for 'interthinking' and the nurturing of a community of practice.

Product oriented

Requiring PSTs to produce written evaluations of their teaching is a common feature of all ITE programmes. This task is reported to develop classroom observation skills (Alger, 2006) and provide the data for the subsequent analysis and reflection on practice (O'Connell and Dyment, 2011). Through the construction of their account and interpretation of what they believe has taken place, the author brings something of themself and may reveal their own personal beliefs and assumptions regarding teaching and learning, a crucial starting point for the process of 'framing' and 'reframing' (Schön, 1983) of classroom incidents. The case studies show that the PSTs found the production of edited videos to be a more valuable evaluation task than drafting written accounts.

Impact of microteaching on classroom practice

A key indicator of the value of any ITE activity must be its impact on the quality of PSTs' classroom teaching during school placement.

Focus group interviews were held with the 16 pre-service teachers from Case Study 1 after they had completed their annual block placement in a secondary school. The interview questions explored if they felt microteaching had helped them to plan, teach and evaluate their lessons and, more generally, if it had any bearing on their experience of placement. All respondents felt that, as a result of microteaching, they were much better at lesson planning, classroom teaching and post-lesson analysis. There was also a consensus that microteaching had equipped them with skills and attitudes which enabled them to learn more during the course of their school placement. Thematic analysis of the feedback related directly to the use of digital video, as shown in Table 2.3.

Table 2.3 Pre-service teachers' views on how microteaching supported them during school placement

Theme	**Comment**
Lesson planning	*'Microteaching helped me to try and imagine what a lesson plan might **look** like in action'.*
Teaching	*'At times I was more conscious of what the pupils could **see** in front of them – almost an out of body experience – from watching the microteaching videos, so I could try and be more exciting'.*
Evaluating	*'Throughout the lesson I was always trying to **spot** any signs it was going ok or clues that I was beginning to lose them'.*
Confidence	*'I was nervous at the start but I felt ready for it as I'd **seen** myself do it and knew it had been alright'.*
Agency	*'I think the microteaching meant that when I got to school I could hit the ground running. I had a clearer **vision** of the teacher I wanted to be. Without it I would have wasted a few weeks and not have been as far ahead trying to improve'.*

The feedback evidences that PSTs continued to benefit from their experience of microteaching throughout the period of extended school placement later in the year. The video-related activities would appear to, as McGarvey and Swallow (1986, p 46) put it, '*help pre-service teachers to move across the bridge from methods courses to field experiences*'.

IN A **NUTSHELL**

By providing PSTs with the opportunity to teach 'bite-sized' chunks of lessons to small groups of peers within the supportive setting of an ITE institution, microteaching is an effective way to develop novices' first attempts at planning, enacting their plans and evaluating. Within this activity, digital video serves as both a means and a resource for the joint exploration of practice and the construction of understanding. Microteaching enables PSTs to learn from observing themselves and their peers and supports them during the school placement phase of the ITE programme.

REFLECTIONS ON **CRITICAL ISSUES**

- *Microteaching is an activity where PSTs teach short lessons to their peers and receive feedback, usually supported by a video recording. It allows for a focus on issues relating to the practice of teaching, such as presentational and interactional skills, and provides the opportunity to model the process of lesson evaluation, within the supportive and theory-rich context of an ITE setting.*
- *In providing the opportunity to closely view their own and their peer's practice, microteaching invites PSTs to experience practice from the perspective of the pupil and a means to set about exploring the cause–effect dynamic between teaching and learning.*
- *As learning to teach is a socio-cultural activity, microteaching should include tasks which require PSTs to work together to create digital accounts of their understanding and thinking regarding their current and future practice.*

CHAPTER 3 | USING VIDEO TO SUPPORT CLASSROOM OBSERVATION

CRITICAL ISSUES

- *How does video help develop PSTs' 'professional vision'?*
- *How can video be used to draw PSTs' attention to how they may think and feel when observing lessons and appreciate the features of a lesson evaluation?*
- *What are the benefits of using video within activities where in-service teachers model their practice?*
- *How can PSTs learn from watching themselves teach?*

Introduction

The process of learning from video begins with observation. Unless the learner is noticing or at least aware of what is going on in a classroom, almost nothing can be learned about teaching or learning, and 'looking at a lesson' rather than 'lesson observation' is probably a more accurate description of the activity. Mason (2011, p 35) considers noticing to be an intentional rather than a haphazard act comprised of practices '*designed to sensitize oneself so as to notice opportunities in the future in which to act freshly rather than automatically out of habit*'. This chapter explores how video-based observation activities can help teacher educators prepare and prime PSTs to use their observations and classroom experiences as points of reference for their future learning.

Observation and learning

Video's principal affordance is that it provides a virtual observation experience for the learner who can simultaneously be both in the classroom and in an environment where they can watch and replay parts of the lesson as often as they want, either individually or with peers or tutors. The breadth and depth of the learning resulting from classroom observation depend primarily upon the learner's capacity to spot and make connections between the myriad of actions and interactions happening frequently, and often simultaneously, around them. This requires PSTs to have the ability to notice and possess the disposition for thinking and trying to 'see' beyond what they happen to be looking at. Classrooms are complex settings, and what is important may not always be noticed. Video provides the opportunity to pause or replay and so allows the tutor to draw attention to the more tacit happenings and empowers the learner to slow down events to a more manageable pace. However, simply watching videos is not enough. Learners require guidance, and tasks need to be structured; otherwise, *'classroom observations can easily turn into messy, unstructured notes, of little use a few days later'* (Santagata et al, 2007, p 124). Formal classroom observation sessions usually require PSTs to record field notes often prompted by questions. Calandra (2015) cautions that without clear and structured guidance, PSTs are too often drawn towards less important facets of the lesson, resulting in accounts of practice which are mostly descriptive or merely narratives of what happened. However, even with such guidance, lesson evaluations can sometimes be overly descriptive and include limited evidence of analysis. Learning activities which focus on developing observation skills should help PSTs to see *and* to reason and so provide them with the capacity to use the classroom as a resource for their own professional learning.

A pedagogy for developing professional vision

An effective pedagogy for using video should enable PSTs to learn from having the best of all worlds – the detailed reality of the classroom, the knowledge and experience of tutors and the support and empathy of their peers. The activities designed around the use of video on campus should exploit the potential synergy between being *helped* to notice and being *supported* in analysis. A pedagogy for the effective use of video within ITE can be informed by Goodwin's (1994) notion of 'professional vision' and Sherin's (2007) research on the use of video clubs within professional development programmes in the USA. Goodwin (1994) uses the term 'professional vision' to explain why an archaeologist can see a collection of stones as part of a larger structure or how a meteorologist can look at the sky and recognise patterns in the shape and colouring of clouds. Within the classroom, professional vision involves the ability to make sense of what is happening and '*drives where and how the teacher will look in the future*' (Sherin 2007, p 384). Both researchers conceptualise professional vision as involving the ability to pay attention to what is important within a lesson and the capacity to appreciate its full meaning and significance. These sub-processes are labelled 'highlighting' and 'coding' by Goodwin, while Sherin (2007) uses the terms 'selective attention' and 'knowledge-based reasoning'. Like all perceptual processes, professional vision is *'not a passive observation of the world'* but involves the dynamic of '*constantly reasoning about what is seen*' (Sherin, 2007, p 384).

Attending to both of these requirements during the early stages of ITE presents tutors with a significant challenge, particularly given the classroom's complexity, the learner's limited knowledge and understanding of related theory and their lack of experience of being in and learning from a professional setting. While the concept of professional vision and explorations of its development have emerged from studies involving in-service teachers, it can be equally useful in ITE as a way to close the gap between theory and practice. Videos can capture reality and preserve it in all its complexity (Marsh and Mitchell, 2014) and so empower tutors to situate theory within the classroom and to ground the discussions in records of practice (McDonald and Rook, 2015). Lundeberg and Scheurman (1997) use the sailing-related metaphor of classroom practice acting as an 'anchor' when it precedes theory or as a 'guide rope' when it follows. Either way, the tutor can use the video-generated discourse to develop learners' professional-pedagogical vision through *'creating and sharing evidence-based arguments of good teaching practice'* (Rook and McDonald 2012, p 1444).

Using video to introduce classroom observation

Based on their work with video clubs, Sherin and Russ (2015) identified common themes within what teachers talked about after watching short video clips of maths lessons. These themes characterise the nature of the comment (for example, did it describe an event, relate one incident to another, make a judgement) and allow for the classification of *how* teachers were thinking about a lesson into a number of 'interpretative frames'. This enabled the researchers to access what teachers were drawn towards and what their thought processes were as they watched a recording of a lesson and to explore how this changed over the course of a professional development programme. Within a lesson observation activity, drawing PSTs' attention to *how* they are thinking as well as *what* they are seeing may help them distinguish between describing or recounting a teaching episode on the one hand and evaluating it on the other. The following case study describes an activity for doing this.

Case Study 1

The aim of this introductory observation task was to allow PSTs to explore the various nature and forms of their thoughts and reactions to video recordings of practice and to become aware of the differences between the various elements of an account of teaching (eg 'description', 'evaluation', 'generalisation'). The activity was designed to be collaborative and open-ended to ensure that learners felt supported and that their views were both valued and valuable.

A group of 20 PSTs watched a five-minute segment of an unedited video of a teacher introducing a numeracy lesson to a Year 3 class. The video showed the teacher recapping the concepts and activities from the previous lesson and introducing the learning intentions and activities for the morning's session. After watching the video, the PSTs worked in pairs to discuss and make notes in response to the instruction and to 'provide an account of what you saw, thought and felt during the lesson'. After watching the video, the pairs discussed the lesson and fed back their comments to the tutor, who scribed all responses on a flipchart before the video was watched for a second time. The tutor then pointed out comments which were similar in content or theme and then invited each group to organise their comments in line with the four 'frames': 'Narrative', 'Personal', 'Evaluative' and 'Generative,' based on an aggregation of the original list devised by Sherin and Russ (2015) (see Table 3.1).

Table 3.1 Interpretative frames used to classify comments (based on Sherin and Russ, 2015)

Frame	Characteristics	Examples
Narrative	Description of events telling the story of the lesson or recalling events that happened whether related or not.	*'The teacher held up each of the cards and asked the pupils to decide which fraction was the biggest and which was the smallest, before selecting pupils to respond'.*
Personal	Expression of feeling or emotion (surprise, excitement, trepidation) or reference to a personal experience.	*'I thought the pupils were fascinating and this is why I want to be a teacher!'* *'I have seen these cards in the College Library'.*
Evaluative	A judgement or expressed opinion on the value or success of a teaching action.	*'The first few cards were easy and then he showed a much harder one which lost them all'.* *'He didn't give them enough time to answer'.*
Generative	A generalisation or sweeping statement based on something in the video.	*'Some pupils need more clues or a bit of help with the answer'.* *'It's good to let the pupils know what they will be learning at the start of the lesson'.*

The tutor then discussed the characteristics of each type of comment and how they might feature within a lesson evaluation. During the next session with this group, the tutor showed a longer (10-minute) unedited recording of the middle section of the lesson where the teacher was using Lego bricks to model equivalent fractions. As they watched the video, the students individually made notes, again on what they saw, thought and felt, and then tried to match each of their comments to one of the four frames. The PSTs then re-watched the video and discussed and compared their notes with their partners. The tutor then led a group discussion of how interpretative frames could assist lesson analysis and invited feedback from the PSTs on this learning activity.

Analyses of PSTs' feedback and written accounts highlight the merits of the activities.

- PSTs realised that they had missed many key incidents during their first observation and that they observed more after re-watching.
- PSTs made connections between incidents and, when reminded of items which they had missed, were able to recall another possible related item.

- Discussion with a partner and then as a group helped reassure them of the significance and validity of their observations and comments.
- Hearing everyone's views, particularly when different to their own, made them think again and more deeply.
- Commenting on feelings such as surprise or excitement allowed for a helpful discussion about how they might react to live observation and served to reassure and motivate learners.

This introductory activity therefore proved effective at making PSTs aware of how they were thinking during lesson observation and showed them the benefits of sharing their thoughts and ideas.

Reflection

- How do you currently use video recordings within your practice?

Video and the modelling of practice

At the beginning of the chapter 'The Power of Modeling' in his book *Slow Teaching: On finding calm, clarity and impact in the classroom*, Jamie Thom (2018) identifies modelling as the most powerful lever for learning. He describes modelling as '*beautiful in its slow simplicity: it is the process by which we make everything explicit*'. The following case study describes how video may be used to complement an in-service teacher's modelling of lesson planning, classroom teaching and lesson analysis, during an observation visit for PSTs.

Reflection

- What strategies do you use to help PSTs transfer visible practice to written plans?

Case Study 2

This series of activities, carried out on campus and in a partner secondary school, aimed to help PSTs:

- develop their classroom observation skills (while in the classroom);
- understand how the content of a lesson plan translates into classroom teaching;
- consider how to go about the process of evaluating practice.

The project involved six pairs of PSTs (three specialising in secondary mathematics and three in secondary science) and six cooperating in-service teachers from a partnership school. Prior to a scheduled observation visit, a twilight video conference was held between pairs of PSTs and the corresponding in-service teacher with whom they would be placed and whose lesson they were going to observe later in the week. During their online meeting, each in-service teacher discussed what had guided their planning and how the various sub-headings in the written lesson plan related to actual activities or materials which they would observe as the lesson progressed. The teachers also provided contextual information about how the lesson plan related to the scheme of work on the topic and the range of ability groups within the class. The lesson plan had been drawn up by the in-service teacher and the ITE tutor to ensure that it was consistent with the format used by the particular ITE institution. It was forwarded to the PSTs in advance of the meeting.

Following this, the PSTs visited the school and had a brief meeting with the teacher prior to the lesson, where the lesson was outlined and the PSTs had the opportunity to ask questions. The PSTs observed and made field notes during the lesson, which was also video recorded. At the end of the school day, the teacher met with the PST and the tutor and talked through their thoughts on the lesson and responded to comments and prompting questions from the ITE tutor. This evaluation session was also video recorded.

Back at the ITE institution, both video recordings were used for two evaluation tasks. The first required each pair of students to use Windows Live Movie Maker to edit the recording of the lesson into a five-minute video, which included the sub-titles 'Introduction', 'Learning Activity' and 'Plenary'. The task also required them to add annotations to the video corresponding to the relevant headings from the lesson plan, such as 'learning intentions', 'success criteria' and 'key questions'. The next activity was a whole group seminar (all six pairs), during which the PSTs re-watched the recording of the teacher's post-lesson evaluation and engaged in a discussion led by the tutor and guided by the following questions.

» To what extent do you agree with the teacher's comments?

» What were the strengths of the lesson?

» Were there any areas for development?

» How did the teacher go about the task of analysing their teaching?

At a concluding seminar the group watched each other's short videos and provided feedback. The group then discussed what they felt they had learned during the activities and if it had developed their understanding of planning and evaluating.

The PSTs considered the following features of this series of activities to be particularly helpful.

- The pre-lesson meeting developed their understanding and appreciation of what the teacher was aiming to achieve in that single lesson.
- Talking through the lesson plan helped the PSTs to appreciate the structure of the lesson, the sequence of events and how the teacher's role changed as the lesson progressed.
- Seeing the lesson unfold, along with the written lesson plan, helped *'to bring the lesson plan to life, to see what the bits meant in real life'* (quote from PST).
- Recording the lesson allowed the PSTs to focus on observing and eased the pressure to make notes on everything that was happening.
- Comparing what the teacher identified as strengths and areas for development to their own views was reassuring and helped them to develop *'an idea of what you should be aiming for and what to look out for during the lesson'* (quote from PST).
- The editing task, although challenging, required repeated viewing, which often revealed more about classroom events and their sequence.
- The opportunity to watch the video of both the lesson and the teacher's post-lesson analysis meant both sources of knowledge and information could be *'slowed down, so then I could understand fully what the teacher meant in his analysis'* (quote from PST).

This case study shows that video can serve as a scaffold for learning *about* practice *from* practice by complementing PSTs' first-hand classroom experiences with video replay and providing them with the opportunity to interact with the recorded practice.

Observing the lesson unfold, both live and again through video, helps PSTs to see how the text translates into action and how enactment appears in a drafted lesson plan. Paivio (1990) uses 'dual coding theory' to explain how video provides additional information not available in text, leading to a difference in the way information is processed by the learner. This use of a video recording in a local classroom, which is the same or a very similar setting to where the PST will be teaching, also eases the transition into practice and helps situate learning and adds authenticity. Santagata and Guarino (2011) reported that PSTs expressed a disconnect with over-edited videos, which gave the impression of being staged and appeared inauthentic. The use of *'real classrooms and teachers with real life decisions and dilemmas'* is particularly useful for PSTs (Marsh and Mitchell, 2014, p 405). The situated knowledge and background information provided by the class teachers help offset concerns about discussing practice when it is removed from its context and the practitioner (Boud, 2006).

Using video for the objectification of self

One of the earliest studies of the impact of using video within teacher education involved PSTs watching recordings of their own short lessons (Olivero, 1965). The study found that PSTs developed their practice much faster when a video was used alongside feedback from their tutor. There have since been many studies evidencing the advantages of using video for self-observation (eg, Calandra et al, 2014; Baecher and Kung, 2011) and much discussion about why and how PSTs learn from observing themselves. Shifting the focus of the camera and the exploration onto oneself ensures that the level and context of practice is aligned to the current level of competence and the practice setting of the learner. It also provides an 'activating experience' (Seidel et al, 2011) and nurtures and sustains intrinsic motivation (Deci and Ryan, 1985). Without viewing videos of themselves, Yadav and Koehler (2007, p 358) caution that PSTs would continue to '*view classroom episodes with their prior lenses*'. However, this personalisation of practice also presents challenges. Eraut (2000) suggests that when watching oneself, the viewer may unconsciously develop a 'deceptive discourse' to reconcile the social need to talk about work with the desire not to give anything away that might lead to being criticized. Amobi (2005, p 129) acknowledges the challenge of getting PSTs to '*risk vulnerability*' by owning up to errors. This personal assessment is crucial as Rosaen et al (2008, p 349) point out '*explicit noticing is critical to change because if a person does not notice, they cannot choose to act differently*'. However, any discomfort on viewing one's own lesson can act as the catalyst for change, or as Bolton (2010, p 9) puts it, '*the pearl grit in the oyster of practice and education*', and concurs with Paley's (1986, p 123) view that '*real change comes only through the painful recognition of one's vulnerability*'. The analysis of self can be initially uncomfortable and requires ensuring PSTs feel sufficiently secure and in their 'comfort zone' to honestly discuss their practice. (Chapter 5 looks at using video to develop reflective practice.) The following case study looked at how the use of video impacted how PSTs evaluated their own teaching.

Reflection

» How do you model the process of evaluating your own practice?

Case Study 3

A group of 18 PSTs in the final year of their four-year BEd programme (primary education) worked in pairs to co-plan, co-teach and co-evaluate a series of six weekly lessons in a local primary school. They recorded videos of each other's teaching on Weeks 2 and 4. A post-lesson evaluation was written by each PST after lesson 2 and emailed to their tutor within 24 hours. A second evaluation was written after each pair had watched and discussed the recording of their lesson, and this was forwarded to the tutor. Based on their evaluations, they each identified an area for development and drafted an action plan involving discussions with each other, their ITE tutors and their class teacher, as well as the use of programme notes and literature. Lesson 4 was recorded and viewed by each pair of PSTs. The final evaluation task required each pre-service teacher to produce a short edited video (using Windows Moviemaker) of lessons 2 and 4, showing the area which they had identified before and after they had developed it and to include annotation to highlight how they felt their practice had improved over the two lessons. Each PST presented their video and shared their experiences with the rest of the group. Data relating to the impact of video and the PSTs' experiences were obtained by questionnaire (N = 18). Six months later, following the completion of their school placement, three groups of the PSTs (N = 15) participated in a focus group interview with the course tutor.

A thematic analysis of the post-lesson evaluations written before and after watching the video showed that they were different in the case of every PST (Figure 3.1).

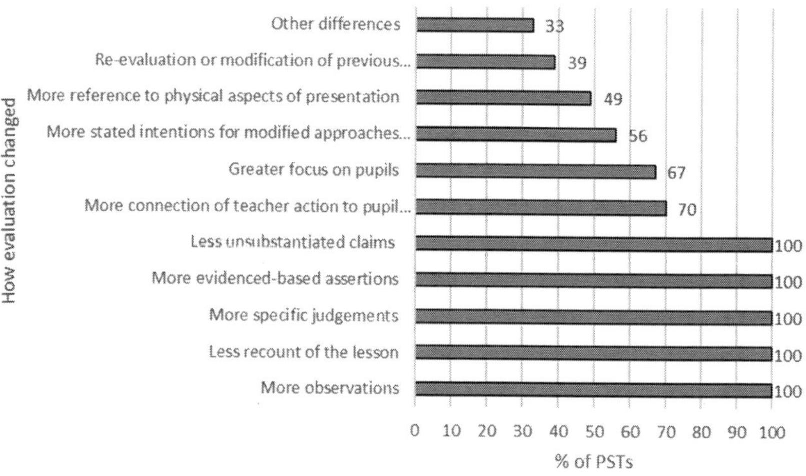

Figure 3.1 How watching the recorded video altered PSTs' post-lesson evaluation

As well as including more observations, the comments and assertions written after watching the recording were more specific to classroom events, evidence-based and less descriptive. Watching and discussing the video also seems to have brought greater clarity to thinking and to have developed a more forward-looking and proactive mindset as indicated by the extracts from the evaluations written before and after viewing the recording (Table 3.2) The longer-term benefits were further evidenced by the focus group interviews (N = 15) conducted later in the academic year and after the completion of their school placement. All PSTs reported that they had benefitted greatly from the experience of watching themselves teach. There was a consensus that the experience of using video had helped them tune in to what they could notice during the course of a lesson and to be mindful of what they might also have missed. It also helped nurture a capacity for evaluation and an appreciation of the importance of evaluation and reflective thinking.

Table 3.2 How video changed the content of post-lesson evaluations: some examples

Change in evaluation	Comment before	Comment after
Re-evaluation of incidents	*'I feel it was a bit rushed at the end but I feel the learning objectives were met and was happy they knew the difference between the words clear transparent and opaque'.*	*'When I watched the video I could really see how my questions only included five pupils. I could see they looked distracted and I had not got everyone's attention for this very important bit. I need to manage my time better and think how to involve them more in the plenary'.*
Strengthening of convictions	*'My explanations of the activities could be improved – in future I aim to improve this aspect of my teaching'.*	*'From watching the video I was clearly able to see that although my explanations of the activities were effective I could have furthered this by modeling what I wanted the children to do and use a picture to show them'.*
Clearer intentions for future practice	*'The questions I was asking I feel were not clear enough leading pupils to answers which were off-topic and not what was needed in the lesson'.*	*'I could really see how I was unable to make use of all the various ideas, one such incident when a pupil gave what could be deemed as an incorrect answer was particularly alarming. Answers which were deemed as "not what I was looking for" should be dealt with in a more positive manner; this would increase classroom participation and pupils would be encouraged to try without fear of incorrect answers'.*

Video and distancing from 'self'

Video not only lets us see more closely into our classrooms but also gives us access to ourselves. It allows for the closer examination of our practice, particularly the contribution of 'self'. This 'private curriculum' (Hamachek, 1995) includes our beliefs, values, style, preference and personal history. A teacher's 'self' influences their interactions with pupils and how they think and act, in ways and to extents which they are unaware of. Chak (2006) believes that this 'self' should be the object of reflection as much as the more public targets of curriculum design, classroom events and teaching strategies. Through observing one's thoughts, emotions and actions (self-observation), information about various aspects of self may be brought to one's awareness. This information can then, as with any other aspect of practice, be reflected upon and interpreted. Chak (2006, p 36) proposes the concept of 'distancing' oneself as a strategy for 'stepping back', describing it as being '*analogous to the image of a person simultaneously split into two roles; self in action and self as observer*'. In capturing the self in action, video supports the process of distancing by separating the action from observation and attends to Sigel's (1993, p 143) description of distancing as '*the psychological separation of the person from the immediate on-going present*'. By engaging in post-lesson self-observation, a PST will be more aware of how they may be likely to react in a future situation and better prepared to seek alternative approaches as deemed appropriate. Therefore, this 'reflection-on-action' has the potential to strongly influence the more challenging (Chak, 2006) 'reflection-in-action'. This strengthening of the synapse between the present and the past was noticed by Eilam and Poyas (2009, p 105), who used video recordings of classroom scenarios with PSTs. They found that the experiences observed in the video '*serve as effective cues activating previously constructed knowledge and thus making it easily retrievable*'. In supporting observation of self, video helps us get more closely in touch with how we act and behave across various situations. We approach future situations more familiar with ourselves in action and therefore better equipped to consider alternative approaches.

IN A **NUTSHELL**

Learning from observation requires the ability to notice and reason as to what and why something may, or may not, be happening in a classroom. Digital video allows for the complexity and tacit nature of practice to be slowed down, replayed and discussed with others. The use of video to develop observation skills should progress from initially learning to observe and understand the practice of others (using a video as a 'window') before being used as a 'mirror' for the development of our own practice.

REFLECTION ON **CRITICAL ISSUES**

- *Video provides tutors with a resource to help PSTs notice the salient features of classroom activity and a means for them to engage in knowledge-based reasoning.*
- *Activities where PSTs discuss how they feel and what they are thinking when watching recordings of lessons can help them appreciate the key features of effective evaluation.*
- *The recording of PSTs' live classroom observation activities, where in-service teachers model planning, teaching and evaluating, allow for a more thoughtful and deeper learning experience.*
- *Video recordings of their own teaching provide PSTs with a clearer appreciation of which areas require development and allow for a greater focus on pupil learning.*

CHAPTER 4 | FROM PASSIVE TO ACTIVE LEARNING
Interacting with video

CRITICAL ISSUES

- *What do we mean by active learning?*
- *How can PSTs interact with digital video?*
- *How and why does interacting with digital video help PSTs to learn?*

Introduction

While a picture may be better than a thousand words, merely watching video recordings of teaching is unlikely to develop understanding. PSTs, particularly those in the early stages of their study, require support and a '*high degree of scaffolding*' (Baecher and Kung, 2011, p 16) as they do not have the knowledge or experience to learn from passively watching classroom footage (Brophy, 2004; Calandra and Rich, 2015). This chapter considers how the facility to pause, rewind, annotate and edit can make the process of learning to teach more active and help teacher educators address the age-old challenge of 'tell me and I forget, show me and I remember, involve me and I understand'.

Active learning

The advantages of adopting teaching practices, which facilitate active learning, relate as much to the pedagogy of ITE as to classroom teaching. While you will be familiar with the principles and rationale for active learning, John Dewey's (1916, p 46) well-known comment is worth consideration.

Why is it that, in spite of the fact that teaching by pouring in, learning by passive absorption, are universally condemned, that they are still so entrenched in practice? That education is not an affair of 'telling' and being told, but an active constructive process, is a principle almost as generally violated in practice as conceded in theory. Is not this deplorable situation due to the fact that the doctrine is itself merely told? But its enactment in practice requires that the school environment be equipped with agencies for doing … to an extent rarely attained.

Dewey points to the need for 'agencies' in the learning environment, which will support active learning. Before considering how interacting with digital video can facilitate active learning, you need to consider what makes learning 'active'. Though it is difficult to provide a specific description of active learning (Prince, 2004), Watkins et al (2007) consider it to have three distinct dimensions.

1 Behavioural – the active deployment and the creating of resources and learning materials.
2 Cognitive – deliberate thought about experiences in order to construct knowledge.
3 Social – learning through talk during a collaborative resource-orientated task.

The emphasis on both 'doing' and 'thinking about' tasks are common features of other descriptions (Zweck, 2006; Snyder, 2003). Active learning pedagogies take the constructivist view that thinking about education should be more centred on learning than on teaching and that learners construct knowledge personally and socially (Freire, 1993; Wertsch, 1997). This requires a learning environment where tasks are intrinsically motivating and offer the learner a certain level of self-directedness so that as learners' capacity increases they become responsible for both the content and the process of learning (Cattaneo, 2017).

The facility to access and interact with a range of recordings of teaching empowers PSTs to be more pro-active in their approach to learning. Active learning is considered to increase motivation and knowledge retention and help learners apply knowledge in other contexts (Michael, 2006; Norman and Schimdt, 1992). The increase in motivation is considered to arise from the learner's freedom of action and opportunity for choice (Drew and Mackie, 2011).

Video analysis tasks

Baecher (2020) proposes a micro-ethnographic approach to video analysis, which focuses on the interactions, particularly the discourse, between humans in social situations (Baker et al, 2008). The transcription and classification of interactions can reveal recurring features and hidden patterns of teacher and pupil behaviours, enabling the viewer to '*see the world in a grain of sand*' (William Blake, quoted by Baecher 2020, p 69). This requires PSTs to extract the data or evidence from the video before considering and discussing it, therefore making them less inclined to jump to unsubstantiated conclusions or rush into making evaluations. This objectification of practice shifts PSTs' focus from the *teacher* to *teaching* and portrays video-based evaluation as less judgemental (Baecher, 2020).

Baecher (2020) describes a number of 'video analysis of teaching' (VAT) activities which could be used within professional development programmes for in-service teachers. Table 4.1 shows how these and similar tasks could be adapted and used within ITE.

Table 4.1 Video analysis tasks for PSTs (developed from Baecher, 2020)

Focus of observation	**Activity**
Teacher talk	PSTs transcribe verbatim the teacher's talk during a short period of the introduction or plenary and then classify the content into categories (eg previous/current subject knowledge, task instruction, classroom or behaviour management). Group sharing and discussion is led by the tutor.
Teacher behaviour	PSTs record teacher's position in the classroom and the use of hand or facial gestures over a section of the lesson.
Teacher pupil dialogue	PSTs transcribe verbatim teacher–pupil dialogue and classify (eg 'affirmation', 'correction', 'development', 'praise'). Group sharing and discussing is led by the tutor.
Pupil behaviour	Each PST records and describes the behaviours of one pupil throughout a short part of the video (eg listening to teacher or other pupil, on/off-task activity, writing, where pupil is looking, responding to question from the teacher, enthusiastic/neutral/disinterested, anxious). PSTs compare their observation records.
Lesson timing	PSTs work individually or as a group to record the sequence and the duration of each stage of the lesson.
Pupil attainment	Individual PSTs record the time of incidents where a pupil displayed knowledge or understanding within each section of the lesson.

Case Study 1 describes how PSTs learned from watching videos and producing written records of pupils' behaviour during a brief lesson in a Foundation Stage setting.

Case Study 1

During their paired placement in a reception classroom (five-year-olds), two undergraduate PSTs, in the second of their four-year degree course in primary education, video recorded the behaviours of two pupils for 10 minutes during their teaching of a short lesson titled 'People who help us'. Following the lesson, the PSTs independently viewed the recording and produced a written time-referenced account of the actions and behaviours of each pupil. They then compared the two accounts and discussed possible connections between the teachers' and children's behaviour. Each PST produced a written reflection on what they had learned from this experience. Key extracts from both accounts are given here.

When I watched and made notes on the video I realised I'd missed quite a lot, and these were pupils sitting close to me! For example, things they said when I was talking to another child or talking to the whole class myself. I could see if the pace of my talking was too fast as they would seem a bit uninterested and when the transition to the activity was too sudden they would be a bit unsettled. I could see how they were responding to my use of language – if the words were too advanced for them. At one point when I was talking about staying safe at night I used the word 'reflection' and on the video I could see it meant nothing to them, and then my teaching partner added, 'the light bounces of your armband' while modelling a ball bouncing back off the wall and going in the direction of her eye, and they were more interested and alert.

(PST 1)

Writing down the time-markers beside their behaviour made us sure we were both talking about the same point in the lesson – we ended up watching it a few times because we did have some things different. It was really good when we both thought the same thing – it made it seem more real and reliable and not just something I alone thought. I had noticed the class really loved it yesterday when I dressed up as a witch, so today I wore my high visibility jacket, and they were so excited and had lots of good stories about it.

(PST 2)

Both accounts show how video analysis tasks require the close observation of pupils' actions and allow PSTs to consider pupil thinking. Philipp et al (2007) looked at how viewing different video content might alter PSTs' thinking about the teaching of mathematics. They found that watching videos of children solving mathematical problems brought about a greater change in PSTs' thinking about the role of the teacher than the viewing of exemplar videos of mathematics teaching.

Interacting with digital video

The various ways in which PSTs can interact with video can be organised around Bouwer's (2011) rubric for the use of video within ITE (Table 4.2). This shows how video interaction can be firstly introduced as an activity to orientate PSTs to classroom teaching and then progressed to support and assess their development.

Table 4.2 Examples of video interaction tasks across the range of video use proposed by Brouwer (2011)

Domain	**Function**	**Video type**	**Focus**	**Form of interaction**	**Learning activity**
Orientation	Introducing and illustrating key features of classroom teaching	Published exemplar	Others	Video annotation using VideoAnt, VLE (eg Canvas), Office 365 Streaming App	• Video annotation – Tutor uploads a video or an exemplar lesson and adds explanatory comments which appear on-screen to identify phases of the lesson or categorise teacher's actions.
	Demonstrating good classroom practice	Published exemplar or locally recorded	Others	Video annotation (as above)	• Video annotation – Tutor uses the comment facility to add questions which require PSTs to evidence their understanding and provide their thoughts and views.
				Video editing using Windows Live Movie-maker (Windows 7 only), Da Vinci Resolve	• Video annotation – PSTs required to respond to annotated questions within each of a number of video clips showing repeated examples of the same teaching practice, for example asking questions, explaining subject content or modelling an activity, lesson introduction or plenary.
				Video Editor and Apple i-Movie	• Video editing – PSTs observe and record a lesson taught by their mentor and create an edited account of the teacher's actions at various stages in the lesson and annotate their account with a theory-informed rationale for the actions.

(*Continued*)

Table 4.2 Examples of video interaction tasks across the range of video use proposed by Brouwer (2011)

Domain	Function	Video type	Focus	Form of interaction	Learning activity
Support	Analysis of personal microteaching	Recording of PSTs' own microlessons	Self	Video editing (as above)	• Video editing – PSTs edit clips demonstrating areas of strength and areas for development and add explanatory text. Edited videos presented and discussed during the seminar.
				Video annotation (as above)	• Video annotation – PSTs add time-marked comments to identify strengths and areas for development in their teaching.
	Provide and respond to feedback on microteaching from peers and tutors.	Recording of peers' microlessons	Others	Video annotation (as above)	• PSTs add time-marked comments and provide feedback to their peers and add comments in response to peers' feedback and questions.
	Develop competence in lesson planning and lesson evaluation	Recordings of published exemplar videos and video recordings of the practice of PSTs from previous ITE cohorts	Others	Video annotation (see above)	• PSTs watch recordings of lessons and work in pairs or small groups to draft a lesson plan. They add time-marked annotations to identify specific connections of teaching to the learning intentions, aspects of classroom management and use of key questions. • PSTs watch recordings of lessons and add annotations to evaluate the lesson under agreed headings (introduction, clarity of presentation, quality of pupil interaction, etc). PSTs use the lesson evaluation template, which will be used during their own placement to draft an evaluation.

	Analysis of classroom teaching	Recording of the first experiences of classroom teaching	Self	Video editing (see above)	• PSTs edit recordings of their teaching to identify the areas of strength or areas for development, or select aspects of their practice to discuss.
Assessment	Formative assessment	Recordings of classroom teaching	Self	Video editing and embedding into PowerPoint presentation	• PSTs edit video recordings of their classroom and combine them with other documents (lesson plan, completed pupil work sheet, lesson evaluation) to create a multi-media record of their planning, classroom teaching and lesson evaluation.
	Summative assessment	Recordings of classroom teaching	Self	Video annotation (see above)	• During PSTs' school placement, a visiting tutor observes a lesson and simultaneously makes a video recording. The tutor provides feedback in the form of time-marked comments and also includes questions and things to think about before sharing the video with the PST. The PST views the video and replies to any questions or prompts with comments and further reflections on their progress (see Chapter 6).

Video annotation

Stevens (2007) provides a compelling rationale for annotation in his account of the use of 'video traces'. A video trace consists of a still or moving image combined with text or an on-screen arrow or drawing, which helps explain what is happening at that precise moment. He argues that these traces are durable immutable objects which allow conversations to be distributed over time and space and allow for explanations or feedback *'to be composed with deliberation while retaining the natural expressive modalities of looking, speaking and pointing'* (p 551). Annotation attends to the interactional nature of learning by bringing PSTs into dialogue with each other and with their tutor. Stevens (2007) suggests that these annotated images take the form of captured 'conversations' which support learning in similar ways to text.

Video annotation as an interactive viewing guide

The use of viewing guides and their impact on PSTs' thinking is discussed and explored by Brouwer and Robijns (2015). Their methodology adopted a 'think-aloud' protocol which analysed the transcribed spoken statements made by PSTs while watching video recordings of their peers' teaching. They found that the use of viewing guides resulted in a greater overall number of spoken statements, with more classified as 'noticing' and 'explanation' and less occurrences of 'acceptance' and 'rejection'.

Video annotation can be used to create 'interactive guides', which guide viewing and thinking and provide a medium through which PSTs can articulate, share and receive feedback on their thinking and understanding of teaching. The process of writing allows PSTs' ideas to be made public and shared (Kellogg, 1994).

Video annotation tools

The use of video annotation has grown in ITE in the past decade (Perez-Tooegrosa et al, 2017), and there are a number of reviews of the various annotation software (Rich and Hannafin, 2009; Rich and Tripp, 2011). Three easy-to-use free options for annotating videos are as follows.

» VideoAnt: A free web-based tool created by the University of Minnesota that allows for time-marked comments and replies to be added (https://ant.umn.edu/).

VideoAnt allows the user to add a comment which is marked on the video timeline. During playback, the comment flashes in the text area of the screen at the corresponding time. Peers or tutors may add comments, responses or questions to this annotation.

» 'Streaming App': Included within Microsoft Office 365

The Office 365 Streaming App does not create a time mark on the video timeline, so the corresponding time can be included in the comment. (The use of the Office 365 Streaming App is discussed in Chapter 5.)

» 'Studio' or 'Arc': a feature on the web-based 'Canvas' virtual learning environment Canvas (https://www.instructure.com/en-gb/canvas). Videos with time markers and comments can be shared within the 'Discussion' area of the Canvas course.

Writing and using annotations

The annotations could take the form of:

» comments or descriptions – '*Notice how the teacher doesn't choose the first pupil with their hand up*';

» specific questions – '*What do you think the teacher is trying to do here?*';

» open-ended questions – '*How does the teacher try and engage all the pupils?*';

» judgements – '*The teacher's writing on the white board is difficult to read*';

» tasks – '*Identify two strengths in this opening introduction*';

» exploratory questions – '*What would you like to ask this teacher about her teaching decisions*?'

Brouwer and Robijns (2015) advise that when writing prompts or comments tutors should focus on the observable features of the lesson, using short sentences in the active voice and present tense. The advantages of using online video annotation include the following.

» The learner has control over pausing and replaying the video.

» The time-marker allows for individual incidents to be accurately identified.

» Pre-service teachers can engage with observation tasks remotely and outside of timetabled seminars.

» The task of writing an annotation or question affords more time for thinking and tends to bring about greater thought than during oral communication.

» Comments and responses are shared across the group and allow peers' responses or comments to be read by the entire group.

» Tutors can monitor responses and comments and thus get a sense of each individual's progress.

The benefits of video interaction

The powerful combination of video and annotation can serve as both a resource and a tool for learning throughout the course of an ITE programme. The *'vividness'* and *'concreteness'* (Brouwer, 2015, p 139) of video focuses learners on the complex interactions between the content of learning, the learner and the teacher, and provides an insight into this '*instructional triangle*'. Yerrick et al (2011, p 132) suggest that digital video provides a '*venue*' for PSTs and tutors to talk through and discuss the more challenging aspects of teaching. In their study PSTs watched exemplar videos of inquiry-based science lessons and used 'Studiocode' software to code the dialogue between the teacher and the pupils. They found that this activity resulted in PSTs adopting a more thorough and evidence-based approach to evaluating their own classroom teaching. The researchers believe that the precision, diversity of views and rigour which coding brings to the analysis of teacher–pupil interaction add to the criticality of the discourse and play a significant role in shifting PSTs' conceptualisations of teaching. The researchers contend that '*without video coding as a tool, confronting preservice teachers' implicit conceptions of excellent science teaching is more of a challenge, as categories and assumptions are rarely explicitly defined. Preservice science teachers needed to have some form of comparison as a control that required them to make defensible claims about practice*' (p 130).

Sherin and van Es (2005) used the software Video Analysis Support Tool (VAST) to develop PSTs' ability to recognise significant features within their practice. Stapleton et al (2017) have also reported similar outcomes using the software Go react.

Annotation for self-evaluation

Video annotation is particularly valuable in the early stages of ITE when potentially vulnerable PSTs attempt to develop what Feiman-Nemser (2001, p 1018) refers to as '*a beginning repertoire'*. The value of using video annotation within microteaching is described in Case Study 2.

Case Study 2

This study evaluated the value of video annotation within microteaching and involved 93 PSTs in the second year of their BEd degree in primary education. Working in groups of three, the PSTs planned, taught and evaluated a short 15-minute science lesson. One member of the group taught the introduction (5 minutes) with the other two members, each teaching the main activity and the plenary (each 5 minutes long). Each group was provided with a digital video recording of their lesson and was required to watch the recording, discuss it and identify strengths and areas for development in both their own and their peers' practice. This took place within a timetabled evaluation seminar during which each student completed an evaluation feedback form.

Working in the same groups, the PSTs planned and taught a follow-up lesson but this time used the online analysis tool VideoAnt to evaluate their teaching and comment on their peers' teaching.

The experience of the PSTs was accessed using a questionnaire after the completion of each of the two cycles of microteaching. Further data were obtained from focus group interviews of four groups, each comprising five participants.

The findings indicate support for the use of annotation (see Table 4.3).

Table 4.3 PSTs' feedback on using VideoAnt

PSTs' views on using VideoAnt	**Yes (%)**	**Not sure (%)**	**No (%)**
I enjoyed using VideoAnt	88	7	5
Using VideoAnt was straightforward	98	2	0
Identifying specific classroom events was better	95	3	2
Annotating required more thinking	92	7	1
Reading peers' comments was useful	99	1	0
Responding to peers' comments was useful	79	12	9
I would like to use VideoAnt again in BEd	77	18	5
I would like to use VideoAnt during placement	66	20	14
I would like to use video during placement	73	21	6

The data from the questionnaire and the focus group interviews indicate that the PSTs had a positive experience of using VideoAnt. The focus group interviews identified the following benefits.

» VideoAnt helped PSTs to appreciate and manage the complex nature of practice.

Although the teaching episodes were very brief the pre-service teachers valued the facility to pinpoint an exact moment in the lesson and carry out a 'micro'-level analysis of their actions.

» Time-marking developed PSTs' awareness of the sequence and duration of activities throughout the lesson.

The use of the time-marker allowed PSTs to notice how the time was apportioned to teacher talk, pupil talk and teacher–pupil interaction.

» Annotating tasks required comments to be more considered and evidence-based.

The task of adding explanatory text required PSTs to think more deeply about their teaching and challenged them to articulate their thoughts more clearly.

» Interacting with the video developed PSTs' sense of agency.

PSTs valued the opportunity to decide which part of the lesson to select for discussion, as one PST stated that he 'liked being in control of what would be analysed'.

Editing digital video

The facility to edit enables tutors to customise videos by selecting key incidents from within or across a series of lessons to illustrate and exemplify the key themes of their instruction. It also provides PSTs with a medium through which they can present evidence of both their understanding and their enactment of practice. Video clips can be complimented by text and images to create digital evidence of attainment.

There are several easy-to-use software packages, including:

- Free Video Editor-(http://www.videosoftdev.com/);
- DaVinci Resolve (https://www.blackmagicdesign.com/products/davinciresolve/);
- Apple's i-Movie.

Tasks can also require PSTs to watch a video provided by the tutor and edit examples of particular teaching behaviours.

The advantages of editing tasks include the following.

- Identifying the precise moment on the video at which to edit the video ensures PSTs watch very closely and more often than they would otherwise do so and therefore can reveal unnoticed incidents.
- The repeated viewing and anticipating of events in the video enhance the viewer's awareness of the sequence of events and phases within a lesson and provide an insight into possible lesson structures.
- It provides another medium through which PSTs can express their views and ideas, for example through presenting and discussing their edited videos during seminars.
- PSTs can use edited videos to evidence their competence in classroom teaching and track their progress and development.
- The sharing of each other's edited accounts of experience across even a small group of PSTs can expose them to a wide range of virtual teaching experiences and increase their subject and pedagogical content knowledge.

Editing provides PSTs with greater control over which clips to include and what comments they want to make. It also ensures that the learning experience is specific to the needs of the individual learner rather than a generic discussion which may not relate to a particular individual. It allows PSTs to accurately recount the story of their personal experience of teaching. For both teller and audience, story-telling can be compelling and emotionally engaging, allowing an individual to reshape, reassess and reconstruct events and create the possibility for change and growth (Williams et al, 2006).

IN A **NUTSHELL**

Digital video provides opportunities for tutors to align recordings of teaching to suit the particular focus of their instruction and to assist PSTs in constructing knowledge and understanding throughout each stage of ITE. Annotation and editing tasks require PSTs to engage in the individual or collaborative deconstruction of practice and the production of valuable learning artefacts. The facility to pause, rewind, annotate, edit and share video provides a resource and the means to learn about practice from practice. Video annotation makes thinking visible and so provides the context and a means for purposeful dialogue.

REFLECTIONS ON **CRITICAL ISSUES**

- *Active learning involves deliberate thinking and interacting with others and resources to create understanding.*
- *PSTs can learn through interacting with digital video by the use of the facility to pause or replay short sections of lessons and create detailed written accounts of teacher–pupil interactions which might otherwise have gone unnoticed or not been fully explored. Annotation software allows for explanatory text to be added by either the tutor or the PST. Recordings of lessons can be edited to select specific incidents and provide a digital account of understanding.*
- *Interacting with video calls for a closer and less passive form of observation and helps reveal the detail and complexity of a situation. Editing and annotation tasks require thinking and the sharing and challenging of ideas with peers.*

CHAPTER 5 | USING DIGITAL VIDEO TO DEVELOP REFLECTIVE PRACTICE

CRITICAL ISSUES

- *What is reflective practice, and why is it important in ITE?*
- *Why can developing PSTs' reflective practice prove challenging?*
- *How can digital video help introduce PSTs to reflection, and how can it progress their reflective thinking throughout ITE?*

Introduction

Engaging in reflective practice is generally considered to be a core standard and benchmark within the teaching profession and a cornerstone of ITE programmes. The concept and practice of reflection provide teachers with the means and a structure to build understanding and construct meaning from within a teaching scenario. During ITE, it provides PSTs with the opportunity to apply and explore their understanding of theory within the classroom. Given that the pre-service phase of teacher education constitutes a very small fraction of a total teaching career, it is vitally important that PSTs develop the facility and the disposition to think reflectively so that they continue to adapt and develop their practice throughout their professional lives. It is reflective practice which makes the difference between '*20 years of teaching experience*' and '*one year of experience repeated 20 times*' (Bolton, 2010, p 8). This chapter looks at how digital video may overcome some of the challenges faced by teacher educators in their efforts to help PSTs become competent and positively disposed with regard to this vital aspect of being a teacher.

What is reflective practice, and why is it important in ITE?

In '*Reflective Practice for Teachers*', Sellers (2017, p 2) defines reflection as '*the deliberate, purposeful, metacognitive thinking and/or action in which educators engage in order to improve their professional practice*'. It is a core competence which enables teaching professionals to fulfil their '*responsibility to the continual development of practical knowledge*' (Bousted et al, 2011, p 10). A constructivist view aligns reflection with the building of knowledge from interpretation (Alger, 2006; Taggart and Wilson, 2005) and provides the means for development and growth as it '*allows for synthesis of understanding into a personal and world view*' (Canning, 1991, p 20). Reflection may also be considered to ease concerns regarding any perceived gap between theory and practice (Goodnough et al, 2016; Korthagen et al, 2001; Korthagen and Kessels, 1999) within ITE programmes.

Studies and discussions of reflection have mostly evolved from Dewey's (1933) seminal work 'How We Think' and his description of it as '*the active, persistent and careful consideration of any belief or supported form of knowledge in the light of the grounds that support it and the further conclusions to which it tends*' (p 9). Dewey's prescription for active and deliberate thought is central to Schön's (1983) view that reflection represents the framing and reframing of practice within the specific context of the classroom situation. The complex nature of practice and the fact that problems can change and are rarely quickly resolved have led to a view of reflection as a cyclic process (Clarke, 1995; Stanley, 1998; Korthagen and Kessels, 1999) which teachers engage with over a period of time.

Why can developing PSTs' reflective practice prove challenging?

Despite its '*allure ... as something useful and informing*' (Loughran, 2002, p 33), ensuring that PSTs adopt a reflective approach to their practice, can prove challenging for a number of reasons.

Reflection can seem vague and abstract

Although the terms 'reflective practice' and 'reflection' are used frequently within the educational literature, their particular meaning can vary from author to author and a general consensus of what these terms mean can be elusive (Zeichner and Liston, 1987; Sparks and Langer, 1992). Rogers (2002a) believes that the absence of a clear notion of what distinguishes reflection from other types of thinking and the lack of a means for identifying and assessing it in action can lead to it being too easily dismissed or taken for granted. Without specific criteria, reflection becomes difficult to engage with and any sense of progression may be hard to identify. Rogers (2002a, p 843) goes as far as proposing that '*in becoming everything to everybody, it (reflection) has lost its ability to be seen*'. Spalding and Wilson (2002, p 1393) suggest, '*We must actively teach and model reflective skills in a variety of ways if we are to demystify reflection*'.

Limited time and opportunity

Hatton and Smith (1995) attribute the barriers to promoting reflection among PSTs to their limited conceptions of the work of a teacher and their preoccupation with coping with their current situation. Unless time and support for reflection is built into school placement, PSTs may focus more on '*what should I do next*' rather than '*why am I doing it?*' (Parsons and Stephenson, 2005, p 103).

Competing priorities

Larivee (2008) points out that despite the prominence of reflective practice within professional standards, the pressure to meet imposed standards of pupil performance can result in practice which is more focussed on expediency and efficiency and less informed by reflection. Time constraints (Copeland et al, 1993) and a crowded curriculum (Davis, 2003) can prove to be insurmountable obstacles. Ng and Tan (2009) point out that reflection can be mistaken for 'sense-making', which looks for a plausible, feasible interpretation consistent with other information and fails to challenge underlying assumptions or beliefs. Extended periods within a school culture where reflective practice is less prominent may restrict the extent to which PSTs question both the efficacy and the value of all that they observe. How they are directed to teach while in school may also restrict their professional growth.

Format for reflection

The worth of requiring pre-service teachers to provide written reflections or reflective journals has been questioned by Hobbs (2007), who questions whether these accounts are either valid or genuine. These written assignments were found to be influenced by whether or not the assignment was being assessed, with students writing what they anticipated the tutor was requiring. However, Fernsten and Fernsten (2005) affirm that reflective skills are best developed within a safe and supportive environment where reflective tasks do not form part of the assessment rubric. Hatton and Smith (1995) raise the issue that judgements and perceptions of students' reflective practice and analysis based solely on their written accounts can only be as reliable and as accurate as each student's ability to articulate clearly their thoughts and actions. Reflective writing is a genre quite different from the more familiar academic style appropriate for essays, so students may feel less comfortable expressing themselves in this personal, explorative and often indecisive form. The danger that the regular and routine use of reflective journals may result in reflective practice becoming superficial, bureaucratised and sanitised is highlighted by Gleaves et al (2008).

Evidence of its value

As the benefits of reflection are often not immediately visible, PSTs may fail to realise them. Ward and McCotter (2004, p 246) suggest that that '*the missing link*' for reflection is a '*tool for the comprehensive assessment of reflection that gives shape to the general principles of reflection, helps teachers visualize how reflection can improve their practice, and explicitly links reflection to student learning*'.

Nurturing and promoting PSTs' reflective practice

A number of studies (Husu et al, 2008; Lee, 2005; Korthagen and Vasalos, 2005; Hatton and Smith, 1995; Lee, 2005; Alger, 2006; Lee and Loughran, 2000; Pedro, 2005; Ottesen, 2007; Rocco, 2005) have shown that with guidance and support, the reflective practice of both pre-service and in-service teachers can be enhanced. This usually involves the use of a series of prompts or questions which provide a structure or a template for reflective journals or written accounts. Alger (2006, p 287) however argues that '*having the skill*' to reflect may not result in PSTs '*doing the skill*' and urges a greater concentration on nurturing a positive disposition to reflection rather than solely on developing the routine. Hobbs (2007) recommends giving pre-service teachers a greater say in the design or format of reflective assignments.

How video can promote reflection within ITE

While strategies and formats for nurturing and recording reflective practice may be disputed, Rosaen et al (2008, p 347) point out that '*the idea of learning from reflecting on one's memory of teaching a lesson is rarely questioned*'. Our memory cannot always be reliable. Crucial details and subtleties of context can often remain unnoticed or may be misinterpreted. Roth (2007, p 368) points out that teachers' recollections of classroom events are changed by time and the filter of intentionality and uses Derrida's (1995) description of experience as something which '*is not recorded in the human body and mind as an indelible trace but takes the character of cinder*'. Video captures the experience and provides the canvas on which PSTs can frame and reframe their thinking about it. How digital video can address each of the challenges outlined earlier is shown in Table 5.1.

Table 5.1 How digital video can overcome the challenge of developing PSTs' reflective practice

Possible barrier to developing PSTs' reflective practice	**How can digital video support this?**
Reflection may seem an abstract, vague and 'fuzzy' concept rooted in the past.	The video tasks engage the learner in specific, purposeful activity and draw them into the cycle of reflection. Reflection becomes something you 'do' as well as how you 'think'.
Time and opportunity are limited during busy placement.	Digital recording extends the shelf-life of lived experience and transforms conceptions of reflection from an 'on the job' footnote to practice to a bridge towards the next practice. Sharing recordings and feedback from others avoids a sense of isolation and the danger of a 'lone scientist' approach.
Focus on school standards and school culture.	Online and on-campus collaboration with tutors and peers ensures reflection is introduced and nurtured within a theory-rich supportive environment. It offsets the dichotomy of theory and practice.
Format for reflection.	PSTs' edited or annotated video lessons serve as powerful texts and don't rely as heavily on the clarity of writing as do written reflections. Digital reflections are seen as different and less routine than other writing tasks.
Evidence of the value of reflection.	PSTs can directly see any progress in their teaching and the impact on pupil outcomes and therefore develop an appreciation of the value of reflection.

Classrooms and schools are busy places, so video recordings offer the opportunity for reflection at a time and place more conducive to thoughtful analysis. Hoath (2012, p 21) proposes that this delay allows the PST '*to move beyond the emotional reaction to the situation*' and recommends that when it comes to reflection, '*as a dish serve cold, or at least lukewarm!*' The affective dimension of learning to reflect is further acknowledged by Hoath (2012, p 22), who considers that the most comprehensive and accessible models of the reflective cycle acknowledge PSTs' feelings and emotions, thereby providing a '*vent for that joy or distress*'.

A video-supported model for reflection

There has been a recent growth in the number of studies and reviews on the use of video to develop PSTs' reflective thinking (McFadden et al, 2014; Endacott, 2016; Tschida et al, 2019; Gibbons and Farley, 2019). An effective model for '*reflective practice*' should allow PSTs to '*practice reflection*' in a supportive and authentic setting. If PSTs are to be convinced of its value, they need to gain experience of its benefits.

Case Study 1

A model for developing PSTs' reflective practice

This Case Study aimed to develop PSTs' reflective thinking through a sequence of activities which connected their learning experiences on-campus and in their placement school. A cohort of 95 PSTs in the second year of their BEd degree in primary education followed through each of the activities in both their ITE institution and placement school (see Figure 5.1). The analysis of their micro-lesson was carried out using the Streaming App within Office 365. The PSTs were required to select incidents in the recording which they considered represented both strengths and areas for development in their practice and add time-marked comments. The comments for each selected incident were guided by a three-prompt analysis framework.

» ***Explain*:** What were you aiming to do at this point in the lesson, and why is this important?

» ***Assess*:** How effective has this been?

» ***Modify*:** What could you change or modify for future teaching?

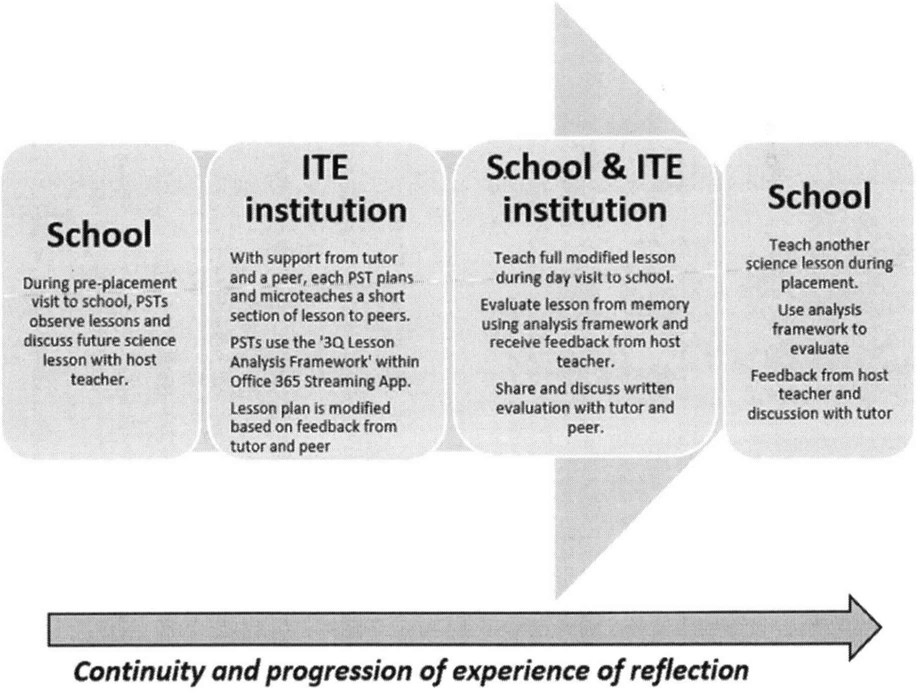

School

During pre-placement visit to school, PSTs observe lessons and discuss future science lesson with host teacher.

ITE institution

With support from tutor and a peer, each PST plans and microteaches a short section of lesson to peers.

PSTs use the '3Q Lesson Analysis Framework' within Office 365 Streaming App.

Lesson plan is modified based on feedback from tutor and peer

School & ITE institution

Teach full modified lesson during day visit to school.

Evaluate lesson from memory using analysis framework and receive feedback from host teacher.

Share and discuss written evaluation with tutor and peer.

School

Teach another science lesson during placement.

Use analysis framework to evaluate

Feedback from host teacher and discussion with tutor

Continuity and progression of experience of reflection

Figure 5.1 A model for ensuring PSTs' experience of reflection is continuous and progressive

Each PST was invited to choose a peer (perhaps a trusted friend or someone focussing on the same topic or pupil age group) who would act as a critical friend for their lesson plan and with whom they would share their online lesson analysis. Based on their own evaluation and the feedback from the tutor and critical friend, each PST modified and redrafted the lesson plan and taught the whole lesson during a visit to their placement school. This lesson was analysed from memory and a written evaluation drafted using the same three-prompt analysis framework. Each host teacher also provided feedback on the lesson and the PST's written evaluation. Back in the ITE institution, each PST shared their experience of teaching and their written evaluation with their peers and tutor during a seminar. During their period of school placement three months later, each PST taught another enquiry-based science lesson and again used the three-prompt analysis framework to evaluate their lesson.

With their consent, data on the PSTs' experience of microteaching and classroom teaching were obtained from questionnaires (N = 49) and semi-structured interviews (N = 12). Follow-up interviews (N = 6) and a focus group interview conducted later in the academic year assessed any longer-term impact.

Overall impact

The Office 365 Streaming App was found to be 'straightforward and easy to use' by 90% of the cohort, and the annotated feedback from peers was valued by over three-quarters of the group.

The data from the questionnaires (Table 5.2) indicate that the analysis framework helped the PSTs to think more and evaluate their teaching. This was supported by interview comments.

Table 5.2 The PSTs' views on the lesson analysis framework

Aspect of evaluation	**Yes (%)**	**Not sure (%)**	**No (%)**
Did the prompt questions make you think more?	96	4	0
Did 'Explain' help you to think and evaluate?	92	2	6
Did 'Assess' help you to think and evaluate?	92	8	0
Did 'Modify' help you to think and evaluate?	100	0	0

- The analysis framework '*showed you how to evaluate'*.
- The questions made evaluation '*more precise and much easier than having to think about the lesson all at once'*.

Analysis structure

Comments show how each analysis question made reflecting easier.

'Explain' – *this was the most challenging as it made you think more deeply as you had to think what the aim was and what you were trying to do at that point and if it fitted with my learning intentions.*
'Assess' – *I needed evidence for this – I had to think of what I noticed or pick up from the class.*
'Modify' – *I think it made the process more forward-looking and valuable as it was about trying to make it better and it wasn't all about being negative.*

Support for planning

In their written account of the experience, 84% of PSTs described how the analysis framework helped to inform their planning and 78% cited a positive impact on their enactment of these plans.

'It made me think and plan in advance the questions I would ask and think to myself, why am I asking them that'.
'I felt a lot more ready and prepared as I was more confident in my lesson plan'.

Support for reflective practice

The data obtained from the PSTs on completing their school placement indicate that the experience had helped them to be more reflective throughout their school experience.

I found this way of evaluating lessons to be simple to complete, easy to understand, and overall a clear way to set out your thoughts on the lesson.

One-third of the PSTs who were interviewed specifically stated that it had made their reflection more 'critical' or more 'effective'.

When I was in school I found myself subconsciously asking the three questions, when I was planning I would think more about what do I want them to learn; and during the lesson I'd be thinking is this working, do I need to change it a bit?

All respondents reported that the experience had enabled them to experience the benefits of reflection and as a result would be more reflective in their future practice.

In a follow-up study, a different group of eight PSTs specialising in secondary science followed the same model (Figure 5.1) with one modification; this time the PSTs video recorded their classroom teaching and so were able to use Office 365 to analyse their classroom practice. This cohort of PSTs also reported that the previous model and the use of the question prompts helped them evaluate their teaching and made reflection easier and more beneficial. All the participants in this follow-up study reported being more reflective during their school placement later in the year.

Discussion of Case Study 1

The three-prompt questions used in Case Study 1 were based on the structure used by Amobi (2005, p 115) to encourage PSTs to reflect on the '*sequence and consequences of their teaching actions*' during microteaching. Amobi's (2005) study found that requiring PSTs to 'describe', 'inform', 'confront' and 'reconstruct' made PSTs think more reflectively. This sequence of thought, first proposed by Smyth (1989), models the process of reflection by guiding PSTs from description to analysis and then, crucially, into action. Balancing description with analysis can prove challenging, as meaning is deeply embedded in context. Smyth (1989, p 13) reminds us that the act of writing itself supports thinking, declaring that '*if teachers create text that comprises the elements of their teaching as a prelude to problematizing it … they will have the basis to discuss and see how their consciousness was formed and how it might be changed*'. The reflective prompts also require PSTs' thinking to be made explicit. The question 'what were you aiming to do at that point in the lesson?' sparks PSTs to compare what is now on the screen with their planned intentions; the follow up 'why is this important?' teases out the beliefs or perspectives on the theory which may have informed their planning. The dialogue with the tutor becomes as much about what and how the PST is *thinking* as what they are or are not *doing*. Rogers and LaBoskey (2016, p 74) assert that for reflection, 'i*f there are no questions, then there can be no energy for inquiry*', and remind us of Dewey's view that 'a *question well-put is half answered'* (Dewey, 1933, p 208).

The findings evidence the value of focussing the microteaching task on classroom practice. The prospect of classroom teaching adds authenticity to the reflective task. The reported longer-term impact on PSTs' reflective thinking suggests this model is effective. Dewey considered experience to be central to learning, as it is a reflection on this experience which leads to growth. He proposed that experience is comprised of the two elements: *interaction* and *continuity* (Rogers and LaBoskey, 2016). Progressing the teaching task from the ITE institution to the classroom and extending the use of the lesson analysis framework brings continuity to PSTs' experience of reflection. The creation and sharing of their annotated videos allow for interaction.

The impact of video on the quality of reflection

PSTs' written accounts of their early teaching experience can be more descriptive than evaluative and therefore may not represent what Davis (2003, p 281) refers to as '*productive reflection'*, that is reflection which '*allows teachers to develop and demonstrate a more complex view of teaching*'. Given the importance of reflection, tutors' role must involve assisting PSTs in '*seeing what matters*' (Davis, 2003, p 281). In previous studies, written or spoken reflective comments have been classified according to 'levels' (van Manen, 1977; Hatton and Smith, 1995; Gore and Zeichner 1991) according to the focus or object of the reflection. Larivee (2008, p 345) believes that reflection is an incremental process and assures '*that even novice teachers can deepen their level of reflection with powerful facilitation and mediation within an emotionally supportive climate*'. This can be achieved by '*providing a more concrete process for assessing a developing teacher's level of reflection [and] can help teacher educators target specific attitudinal and behavioural characteristics necessary for reflective practice*' (p 345). In an attempt to operationally define the three levels of reflection most commonly depicted in the literature, Larivee (2008) sought a consensus from academics and teacher educators who have written or reported on the topic of reflection and identified a set of descriptors or 'practice indicators'. Case Study 2 explores how digital video and Larivee's descriptors could be used to enhance the quality of PSTs' reflections.

Case Study 2

The study involved 22 undergraduate PSTs in the fourth and final year of their BEd in primary education. The PSTs each planned and taught a series of science lessons in a local primary school, including two lessons which were video recorded. Each PST viewed and discussed the recording of their lesson with their peer before producing a written account of the strengths and areas for development in their teaching. Before their next lesson, the PSTs took part in a seminar which introduced the concept of levels of reflection. The seminar used pre-recorded lessons and examples of previous PSTs' reflective accounts to characterise Larivee's (2008) descriptors of each of the levels of reflection (see below). It also included a discussion of the importance of considering how the choice of the camera angle and deciding which parts of the lesson to record have a bearing on what the viewer may evaluate. The PSTs then taught and video recorded another lesson and produced a reflective account as before.

The PSTs' written accounts were analysed and the reflective comments were classified according to Larivee's (2008) levels of reflection.

» Level 1 – pre-reflection: interpretation of classroom situations without thoughtful connection to other events or circumstances.

» Level 2 – surface reflection: focus largely limited to teaching technique.

» Level 3 – pedagogical reflection: connects pupil learning with teaching structures and recognises the role of pupil prior knowledge and importance of engagement.

» Level 4 – critical reflection: questions the worth and value of established teaching practices and challenges assumptions and explores alternative approaches.

The reflective accounts written after the seminar on the levels of reflection contain more reflective comments and a greater proportion of Level 3 comments (see Table 5.3).

Table 5.3 The number and level of reflection of PSTs' written reflections before and after the seminar

Level of reflection	No. evidenced in reflection 1	No. evidenced in reflection 2	Example of written reflection
Level 1 – pre-reflection	6	4	*'The pupils aren't very good at group work so a lot of time was wasted on taking turns with the torches'.*
Level 2 – surface reflection	68	41	*'I should have gone around each table more to make sure everyone was reading the thermometer properly'.*
Level 3 – pedagogical reflection	56	131	*'The puppet really got them excited and they were telling it what should be in his healthy lunchbox. It gave them a reason to talk about what they think'.*
Level 4 – critical reflection	2	8	*'Most of the science they do is really just listening to the teacher and worksheets. They were so excited to get doing stuff'.*
Total	132	184	

Discussion of Case Study 2

Case Study 2 shows that explicit focus on the levels of reflection can help PSTs extend their thinking beyond issues of presentation to consider pupil experience and reaction. Discussing and providing visual examples of each level of reflection helps PSTs to engage meaningfully with their own experience of practice. Rogers (2002, p 232), writing about her professional development work with teachers, acknowledges '*no matter how many good ideas and best practices exist, I cannot "stick them onto" teachers. Without keeping their experience central, I can get no foothold into their learning as teachers*'. The sharing and discussion of videos across the group allow for the comparison of pedagogies and their impact on pupil learning. Now that PSTs can 'see' for themselves, they are ready to examine their own practice and the accepted forms of pedagogy experienced during their time in schools.

It is also important that ITE provides supported opportunities for PSTs to engage in critical reflection, by questioning and challenging taken-for-granted assumptions and practices. Within the more secure setting of their peers and tutors and away from the hierarchical expert–apprentice dynamic, which can characterise and restrict PST professional growth during school placement (Murphy, 2016), PSTs can begin to conceptualise practice as something which can be created. Curriculum innovation and the future development of pedagogy require teachers with the skills and the agency for change. Developing reflective thinking within ITE is also therefore important for the development of future educational leaders (Nahavandi, 2006; Roberts and Westville, 2008).

How video can support the cycle of reflection

The model of reflection as a cycle has been developed in many studies (Kolb, 1984; Korthagen and Kessels, 1999; Gibbs, 1988). While these cycles may vary in the terms used and the number of steps, they follow a similar pattern which draws the user through a sequence of steps towards improvement. For example, Korthagen's (1985) ALACT model comprises: action (teaching); looking back; awareness of essential aspects; creation of alternative methods/solutions; and trial. Digital video can make each of these steps easier and allow PSTs to actually see and realise the value of reflection. Figure 5.2 shows how digital video can support activity throughout Pollard's (2019) cycle of reflection.

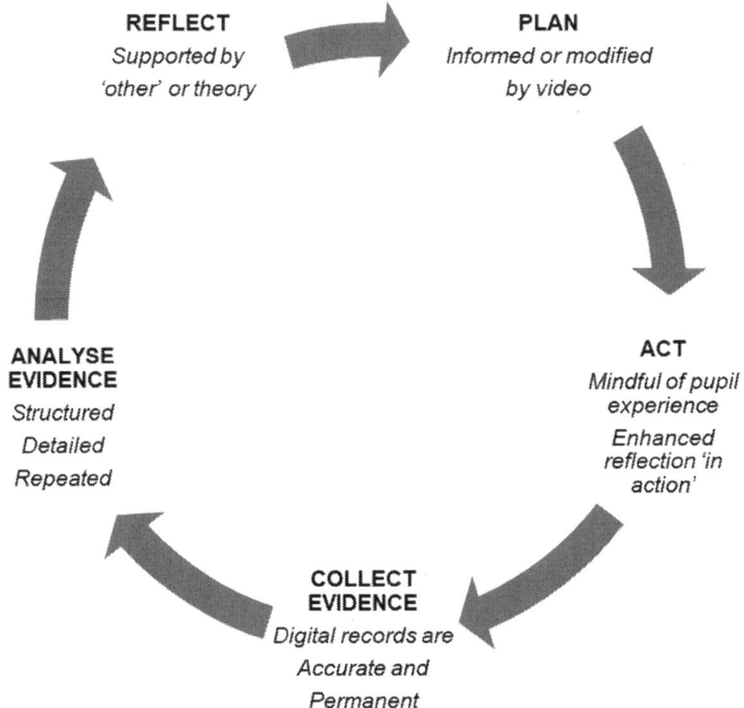

Figure 5.2 Video-supported cycle of reflection (adapted from Pollard's *Reflective Teaching in Schools*, 5th Edition, 2019)

The importance of 'being present' within experience

Rogers' (2002b) model for the reflective cycle begins with teaching and, while similar to Pollard's (2019), it highlights the importance of 'being present' through paying attention and being alive to the needs of the pupil (see Figure 5.3).

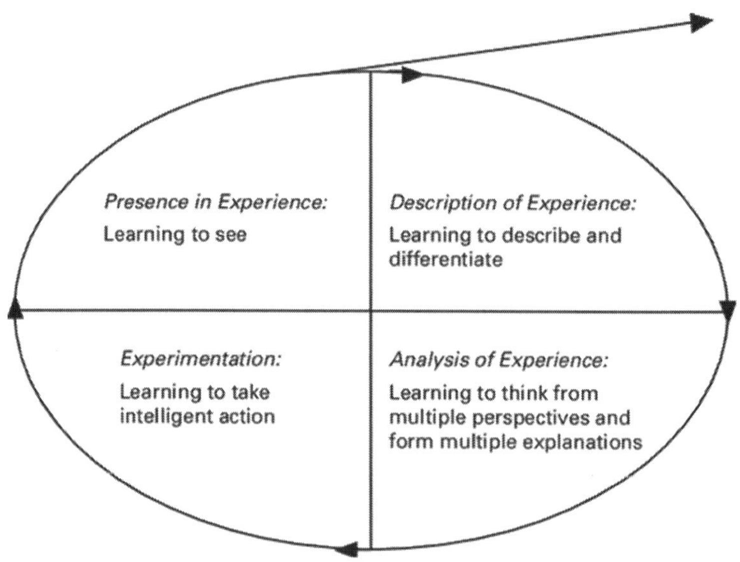

Figure 5.3 Rogers' reflective cycle (2002b, p 235)

The vividness conferred by video's sounds and images can help the viewer to be present again and consider what else they might have attended to. This re-living of their experience draws the PST closer to their practice and helps them remember what they were attempting to do and what they were thinking and attending to as the lesson unfolded. This '*immersion*' and '*resonance*' (Goldman, 2007, p 508) are considered by Seidel et al (2011, p 260) to bring about higher levels of teacher motivation and activation. Rogers (2002b, p 234) views reflection as a form of extended enquiry which '*keeps at bay this tendency to interpret and react to events by first slowing down to see, then describing and analysing what happened, and finally strategizing steps for intelligent action that, once carried out, become the next experience and fodder for the next round of reflection*'.

Rogers' cycle also acknowledges the importance of the 'description of experience' as a preface to analysis. It is the description of experience which Rogers considers to be the most challenging phase as teachers are keen to move on. However, it is '*the discipline of description*' (p 238) which forces PSTs to '*slow down, to look, and to see the variety and nuance present in such moments before leaping into action*'. In her professional development work, Rogers invites in-service teachers to view ambiguous images and videos of teaching scenarios and then produce written descriptions of what each of them has observed. The difference across all the accounts helps illustrate how description is often influenced by subconscious interpretation and helps make teachers mindful of the blurred boundaries between the two components of reflection.

How and why the use of digital video can nurture and develop PSTs' reflective thinking can be considered in light of what Rogers (2002a) considers to be Dewey's founding principles of reflection (see Table 5.4).

Table 5.4 How each of Dewey's principles of reflection (Rogers, 2002a) are supported by digital video

Dewey's principle for reflection	**Role of digital video**
1. Reflection is a meaning-making process which in connecting experiences and ideas ensures continuity of learning and progress.	• Experience can be captured and transferred for 're-living'. • PSTs can experience their own progress.
2. Reflection is a systematic, rigorous process of enquiry-based thinking with action.	• Digital recordings ensure that complexity is preserved, and a thorough analysis is feasible. • Creation of digital artefacts to support and represent learning.
3. Reflection requires collaboration with others.	• PSTs' experience and, crucially, their thinking in relation to that experience can be shared, discussed and annotated with tutors and peers.
4. Reflection requires positive attitudes towards the development of oneself and others.	• PSTs enjoy working with digital video, which is personally and professionally rewarding.

Digital video enables PSTs to make the most of their experience and therefore has the potential to enrich their education. Rogers et al (2021) further reminds us of Dewey's (1916, p 16) view that '*education is that reconstruction or reorganization of experience that adds meaning to experience and increases the ability to direct the course of subsequent experience*' (p 82).

IN A NUTSHELL

Developing the reflective thinking and practice of PSTs enables them to develop their current understanding and enactment of teaching and also equips them with the skills and disposition for career-long professional development. Activities based on digital video can help PSTs to become competent at using their practice as a resource for learning and convince them of its value. Digital video helps PSTs to situate learning within the experience and facilitates purposeful activity through each stage of the reflective cycle.

REFLECTIONS ON CRITICAL ISSUES

- *Reflective practice is the tendency to revisit the enactment of one's teaching in order to think deeply about its effectiveness and value with a view to modify or change it.*
- *Reflecting on practice can be confused with merely thinking about what has happened in the classroom and therefore lack sufficient deliberation and objectivity. Becoming reflective requires guidance and the opportunity to practice within the context of one's own experience. During a busy school placement, PSTs may struggle to find time to reflect and, if not fully convinced of its value, view it as another imposed task and adopt a tokenistic approach.*
- *Digital video enables PSTs' experience to be captured and thoroughly explored. It can help break down reflection into a series of manageable steps and enable learners to see both problems and solutions. Even a brief experience of using video to guide their reflection can have a significant impact on PSTs' future practice.*

CHAPTER 6 | VIDEO AND THE ASSESSMENT OF CLASSROOM PRACTICE

CRITICAL ISSUES

- *How can video be used to enhance the quality of assessment of PSTs' classroom teaching?*
- *How does video alter the role of the tutor or mentor during school placement?*

Introduction

Assessment is a fundamental aspect of learning, serving both as a means for measuring attainment and supporting further learning. Within ITE, the assessment of practice is largely based on a tutor's or a mentor's observation of a PST's classroom teaching over a number of visits to the classroom. Ensuring that this assessment is robust and that feedback is effective presents a number of challenges to teacher educators. This chapter outlines how digital video can be used for both the formative and summative assessment of PSTs' practice and explores how it may alter the role of the observing tutor or mentor.

The challenges of assessing classroom practice

School experience plays a vital role in teacher education programmes as it gives PSTs the opportunity to teach, receive feedback, reflect on their teaching and then teach again. Darling-Hammond (2010, p 40) calls this process '*practice in practice, with expert guidance*'. Providing PSTs with useful feedback requires close observation of instruction, specific commentary and reflective coaching discussions (Stapleton et al, 2017). This can prove logistically challenging for tutors where there is a large cohort of PSTs teaching in many schools. The accuracy and robustness of any assessment of a PST's classroom practice depend on a number of factors.

» How many observations and discussions is it based on?

» Is the practice observed typical of that PST, or are they teaching uncharacteristically above or below their usual level?

- Do the observed lessons represent a range of curricular areas, or are they mostly subject areas where the PST's practice may be particularly strong?
- Has the level of performance been reduced by the PST's anxiety or stress?
- Did the tutor's presence distract the pupils?
- Did the tutor fail to notice, or omit from the discussion, an important incident in the lesson?
- How informed is the observer regarding the context in which the lesson is set, for example prior learning, ability range of the class and behavioural issues?

Furthermore, the focus on summative assessment and awarding of a grade or score may make PSTs disinclined to adopt more challenging teaching methods and opt instead for 'safer' learning activities where they have greater control. This may limit the learning resulting from the feedback discussion.

Case Study 1 describes how video was used to support the assessment of PSTs during their placement in school and discusses its impact on PSTs' learning and the role of the observing tutor.

Case Study 1

Using video to support assessment and feedback during placement

This study sought to explore if using video altered PSTs' experience of a tutor's formative assessment and feedback during their period of school placement within a BEd degree programme in primary education. Within each of the four years of the programme, PSTs spend eight weeks in a primary school where they are required to plan, teach and evaluate a number of lessons. The assessment rubric is based on the General Teaching Council for Northern Ireland's competence model (GTCNI, 2007). The tutor observation visit comprises a pre-lesson discussion on progress, lesson observation and a feedback discussion. Each PST receives a written feedback report, which categorises the PST's practice as 'achieving', 'working towards' or 'limited evidence' in each of 11 competencies. The report also provides qualitative feedback on each of these aspects of practice.

The 10 PSTs who volunteered to take part in the study were in either their first or second year. During their eight-week placement in a primary school, they video-recorded their teaching on a minimum of two and a maximum of four occasions. The duration of each recording was no longer than 20 minutes and could take the form of a single take or a number of shorter video clips. The recordings were uploaded onto VideoAnt, where they watched back their lesson and used the time-mark and annotation facility to identify and comment on the areas of strength and areas for development in their teaching. This VideoAnt analysis was then shared with their tutor and at least one other PST from the group. The tutor watched the video, read the PSTs' comments and then added comments of their own. The PSTs were free to choose which lesson to record and analyse.

Each PST was visited on two occasions by the same tutor who observed and made a video recording of the lesson in addition to following the standard visit protocol. Within 48 hours, the tutor uploaded the recording onto VideoAnt and used the annotation facility to add comments and questions for the PST to respond to. This VideoAnt was then shared with the PST.

On completion of their placement, each PST produced a written reflection in response to the question, 'Do you think receiving video informed feedback helped develop your practice during placement?' Further feedback was obtained from a focus group interview with six of the PSTs. All participants were assured that participation in the study was voluntary, had no bearing on the grade awarded for their school placement and they were at liberty to withdraw from the study at any point. All school principals were briefed on the aim of the project, and parental consent was obtained for recording and sharing videos within the group.

Findings

All the participants reported having a positive experience and felt that video had helped them to learn from the assessment process. A number of the advantages of using video cited by the PSTs have been discussed already in this book and include:

- noticing incidents and aspects of the lesson which were missed during teaching;
- being able to see the lesson from the perspective of the pupils;
- being able to watch a number of times;
- being able to see positive aspects of the lesson and in the teaching;
- being able to closely observe pupil activity and behaviours during the lesson.

The advantages relating specifically to assessment include the following.

- The additional recordings allowed the PST to demonstrate their competence in a wider range of teaching scenarios and across different areas of the curriculum.
- The PSTs could record a lesson where they felt they would like guidance and feedback from the tutor or which evidenced what they considered to be good practice.
- VideoAnt allowed for feedback to be precise.
- Receiving positive feedback and guidance from the early stages of their placement reassured PSTs and made the 'live' visit from the tutor less stressful.

» Viewing the recording of their lesson which the tutor had made, and reading the annotated feedback, helped PSTs fully understand the oral and written feedback which the tutor had provided directly after the lesson.

» The increased communication with the tutor made the experience as much about learning as assessment.

Using video to support summative assessment

Video allows for more lessons to be observed and is, therefore, a more reliable assessment of a PST's competence. During Case Study 1, a minimum of four and in some cases six lessons were recorded (two made by the observing tutor), in contrast to two under non-video arrangements. The tutor re-watched the recordings of the lessons at which they were present and noticed some incidents and teaching actions which were missed during the live observation. This second opportunity to observe the lesson away from the classroom allows for further consideration of how best to feedback and can be informed by additional comments from the host teacher or further examination of the PST's lesson plans and teaching materials. The recordings from all participating PSTs could be compared to ensure that criteria had been applied consistently and marks awarded fairly across the group. Although this case study involved only one tutor, the sharing of videos could be used to moderate grades across a number of tutors, as is the practice when assessing PSTs' written work.

Video also allows for a more accurate assessment of PSTs' ability to evaluate and reflect on their practice. Having reflected on feedback where the tutor identified an area for development, a PST may share the recording of a follow-up lesson where they feel they have acted upon the guidance or suggestions made by the tutor. This sequence of videos allows PSTs to evidence their understanding and application of the cycle of reflection. The additional observation opportunities provided by video also enable tutors to assess PSTs' practice across a wider range of curricular areas. PSTs could be required to share videos of their teaching in particular subject areas, ensuring their competence extends beyond the frequently observed areas of numeracy and literacy. Videos could also be shared with tutors who are specialists in particular subject areas. This could support struggling candidates by helping them connect their classroom enactment with the principles and theory previously covered in other parts of the programme and provide higher-achieving PSTs with the expertise of a specialist tutor.

Formative assessment and feedback

The aim of formative assessment is to provide feedback on performance in order to improve and accelerate learning (Sadler, 1998). Thematic analysis of the PSTs' written reflections identifies the ways in which video promotes learning. The PSTs' comments are consistent with what Nicol and MacFarlane-Dick (2006) consider to be the seven principles of good feedback, as shown in Table 6.1.

Table 6.1 How PSTs' comments on the use of video align with the principles of good feedback (as defined by Nicol and MacFarlane-Dick, 2006)

Principle of good feedback	Number of citations (n = 63)	Percentage of all comments (%)	Pre-service teachers' comments
Clarifies what good performance is	7	11	*When I was evaluating myself at the start I wasn't always sure to what extent what I was doing was a strength or a weakness. When I watched it again with the tutor's comments I could see what he was looking for.*
Delivers high-quality information	18	29	*It was particularly good for seeing pupil behaviour in more detail and how I managed behaviour – the tutor comments made me see I wasn't responding quickly to them – good suggestions for what I might have done.*
Facilitates self-assessment	7	11	*Normally in your evaluation you don't think about your questioning or your dialogue with the pupils, unlike with the video, when you do get a chance to see how useful was that question, how could I have developed that – it was so much more useful than just recalling it all.*
Encourages tutor and peer dialogue	6	10	*It was a great support network; normally you only see your tutor in one or two lessons, but having a VideoAnt for each week was useful and reassuring to get feedback on what was going well and suggestions for other parts. It was good reassurance and good to keep communication going so you knew the tutor was always there to support.*
Encourages positive motivational beliefs and self-esteem	6	10	*When the tutor agreed with my comment I felt good – like my judgements were ok, so I would be inclined to look for more things and add more comments.*

(*Continued*)

Table 6.1 Continued

Principle of good feedback	**Number of citations (n = 63)**	**Percentage of all comments (%)**	**Pre-service teachers' comments**
Provides an opportunity to close gap between current and desired performance	12	18	*The feedback allowed you to confirm your evaluations but also to get further input on what you could improve on in your lessons. Our tutor's comments were very helpful; they were a mix of encouraging and constructive and gave practical advice.*
Provides information to help shape teaching	7	11	*We should be able to use this more and share our VideoAnts with other students in similar classes and get their feedback.*

Nicol and MacFarlane-Dick (2006) propose that in higher education, formative assessment and feedback should be used to empower students as self-regulated learners. Self-regulation when learning to teach requires PSTs to have in mind some conceptualisation of the criteria and standards required in order to set goals and progress towards them. External feedback can help generate internal feedback and help empower PSTs to learn. The PSTs in Case Study 1 valued being able to decide for themselves which lessons they would record and share with tutors.

Feedback is often complex and requires PSTs to actively discuss and construct an understanding of it before using it to improve (Higgins et al, 2001).

Sadler (1989) proposes that in order to learn from feedback learners must:

- have an understanding of what good performance is;
- know how their performance compares to this;
- be able to close the gap between current and good performance.

Nicol and Macfarlane-Dick (2006) point out that PSTs' inaccurate conceptions of goals can divert their activity and compromise the value of external feedback. If both PST and tutor do not share a clear understanding of what may be wrong with practice, feedback is less likely to connect with the learner or create a sense of 'resonance' (Goldman, 2007, p 31). Lofthouse and Birmingham (2010, p 10) report the impact of video on assessment to be, *'as if the "penny drops" as they can actually see and therefore fully appreciate the problem'.*

In addition to providing feedback, post-lesson discussions should try to develop PSTs' self-assessment skills. PSTs need to possess evaluative skills similar to those of their tutors.

Video plays a vital role as it lets PSTs *see as* a tutor and encourages them to *think like* a tutor. Requiring PSTs to provide a critique of their practice, as it unfolds, casts them in the role of the tutor and may help shift the view that formative assessment and feedback are the responsibility of the tutor. The achievement of learners' goals requires learners to take ownership of them (Black and Wiliam, 1998). The development of learners' self-assessment skills has been found to be greatest when both internal and external feedback are provided together (Taras, 2003). This is often difficult to achieve within a busy school setting. The use of VideoAnt, however, allows tutors and PSTs to affirm, challenge or extend each other's comments. Providing feedback to peers further develops self-assessment skills as it requires PSTs to make and refine objective judgements against the same standards which equally apply to their own practice. Napoles (2008) reports that PSTs find feedback more useful when it comes from a number of sources.

The role of the tutor

A number of studies have reported on how the role of the tutor can influence PST learning (Sanagata and Angelici, 2010; Zhang et al, 2010). The use of video-supported assessment described in Case Study 1 can bring about a more productive relationship between the tutor and the PST. The additional 'virtual' observations require more frequent communication and can help establish a shared understanding of the assessment process. Watching a recording of a lesson prior to visiting allows the tutor to tune in to the level of the PST's practice and anticipate the areas and nature of support likely to be required. The online feedback can provide reassurance to the PST and help ease the stress of the first live visit. The discussion during the tutor's first visit can then review the PST's progress on the feedback provided by the previous video. Over the course of this extended number of observation–feedback cycles, the tutor comes to adopt the role of a coach rather than a judge.

Providing useful feedback which will result in learning can present a number of challenges to tutors. PSTs may believe they are performing better than they actually are, and over-confidence and a lack of self-awareness regarding self-efficacy may limit their capacity to self-regulate (Crichton and Gil, 2015). There is a tendency, particularly at the beginning of their studies, for PSTs to assess their effectiveness by what they say or do rather than how their pupils respond (Morris, 2007). Even when watching videos of their own teaching, Sanagata and Guarino (2011) found that teachers can be defensive of their practice. They report that although teachers are activated and motivated by watching recordings of their own practice, they can be less critical and suggest fewer alternative actions than when viewing recordings of others.

Danielowich and McCarthy's (2013, p 157) study of the use of video for the assessment of PSTs' classroom teaching reports how the video allowed tutors to find *teachable moments* to send new messages, or to resend previous ones, in more concrete ways. The tutors also reported the experience had activated their own learning as it '*triggered quandaries about how to offer gentle but effective "in-action" guidance to student teachers and helped them exercise greater stances of inquiry*'.

Learning from high-quality feedback

Video's provision of detailed and specific feedback was highly valued by the PSTs in Case Study 1. The following extract from an interview with a PST shows how she was able to learn more from the tutor visit than would have been possible without video.

I have been struggling a bit with my classroom management of this P2 (Year 1) class. When I'm reading the story they were unsettled and kept shouting out. I was stopping all the time to deal with wee things and found it hard to get much covered. I have tried to follow the advice and do all the things you should, but don't know how to get the balance right. The video was great because I could write in my thoughts and questions at each time I wasn't happy with it and ask 'what should I do here?' and (tutor's name) could say what he thought of what I was doing and make suggestions. His comments were really helpful as he would say what I should be doing as the lesson went on; he suggested moving two boys who were really fidgeting, up to the front to hold the objects for me and this worked; they were listening more and taking part.

This scenario bears the features of situative learning in that it is an authentic experience mediated by social, collaborative activity (Blomberg et al, 2014). It is the minute-by-minute advice and affirmation which makes the difference for this student. The video helps the PST to move from having the knowledge of what she might do (her theory), to actually doing it (enactment), and then allows her to consolidate her learning by observing, reflecting and discussing the benefits. On the tutor's part, though the lesson was observed live, the video provides further time and space to consider how best to advise and guide the PST. It allows the tutor to go beyond the general in their recommendations and to 'go granular' (Bambrick-Santoyo, 2016).

IN A **NUTSHELL**

The classroom provides the venue for the assessment of PSTs' practice and an arena in which they can learn about teaching. Video can enhance the rigour of summative assessment and add considerable value to the process of formative assessment and feedback.

REFLECTIONS ON **CRITICAL ISSUES**

- *Video allows tutors to observe a greater number and wider range of lessons and therefore arrive at a more reliable assessment of the strengths and short-comings in PSTs' classroom practice. The detailed and specific feedback provided by video strengthens the formative nature of assessment and can help PSTs to become more engaged and active in assessing and improving their own practice.*
- *The use of video helps shift PSTs' perception of the tutor from a judge to a coach. The additional observations and communications enable the tutor to adopt a more supportive role in the assessment process.*

CHAPTER 7 | THEORETICAL PERSPECTIVES ON THE VALUE OF USING VIDEO IN ITE

CRITICAL ISSUES

- *How does the use of video within ITE relate to social constructivist theories of learning?*
- *How does using video enhance PSTs' self-efficacy beliefs?*
- *How might video support a better learning environment for PSTs?*

Introduction

The previous chapters of this book describe how and why digital video can support PSTs in their learning journey through the pre-service phase of their teaching career. This chapter explores how a social constructivist view of learning can explain the value of video and how it can enhance PSTs' confidence and assuredness in their practice. It also considers how digital video may enable ITE institutions and partner schools to work more closely for the benefit of PSTs and both parties.

The technological and social affordances of video

Our understanding of the advantages which video offers over other forms of teacher education pedagogy emerges from learning sciences' research and theory which characterise knowledge as constructed, situated, social and distributed (Fishman, 2007; Pea, 1993). Stevens (2007) sees video as representing a '*socio-technical infrastructure for learning that is quite different*' and a means to '*help people become active, critical, makers, revisers, and users of ideas, tools objects and images*'. It is this activity which he proposes overcomes the problem of '*inert knowledge*,' citing Whitehead's (1929, p 1) description as '*ideas which are merely received into the mind without being utilized, or tested, or thrown into fresh combinations*'. Video recordings of lessons represent artefacts which are authentic and '*ecologically valid*', allowing for analysis away from the classroom in '*a more deliberate and considered way*' (Goldsmith and Sego, 2011).

The affordances of digital video arise from the facility to capture and interact with classroom practice (technological affordance) and the means to do so in collaboration with tutors, mentors and peers (social affordance). This technological affordance makes learning easier by reducing the cognitive load (Sweller, 2010). Social affordance has its source in the moral support and guidance provided by peers and tutors. Given that a number of studies have shown that anxiety before and during placement can impede learning (Hayes, 2003; Hurley and Cammack, 2014), it is encouraging that the affirmation resulting from positive feedback from peers or video playback can provide a gentle and supportive introduction to classroom practice.

Digital video as a tool for action

The value of digital video within ITE can be best explored from a sociocultural perspective of learning as a collaborative, developmental and purposeful human activity. Vygotsky (2004, p 83) placed action at the centre of development, stating that '*psychological functions emerge out of social, collective activity*'. When PSTs come together as a group to make sense of their own or others' practice, they are adopting what Stetsenko (2008) describes as a '*transformative activist stance*' with respect to learning to teach. Based on the work of Vygotsky, Piaget and Dewey, Setsenko (2008, p 479) stresses the centrality of collaborative activity within the process of transformation. Learning from digital video enables PSTs to overcome what she describes as '*the spectator stance, through the realisation that the only access people have to reality is through active engagement with and participation in it, rather than simply "being" in the world*'. This activity is considered by Stetsenko (2008) to be '*neither ancillary nor complementary to development and learning; instead they are the "very realm" that these processes belong to and are carried out in*' (pp 479–480).

Digital video activities can progress from initially gathering information as an individual to sharing tasks and ideas with a peer, before engaging in the joint exploration and application of knowledge within the wider community of learners. When used throughout the ITE programme, activities created around video can draw PSTs together and deepen their level of engagement, therefore extending the level of attainment. An extended form of microteaching called macroteaching has been developed and found to be effective by Stroupe and Gotwals (2018), where PSTs engage in what they refer to as 'ambitious science teaching' of their peers over full-science lessons. They report that this macroteaching develops PSTs' confidence in adopting the more challenging pupil-centred approach to teaching science through investigations and, through adopting an enquiry stance to their own ITE practice, adds to the tutor's own understanding of the pedagogy of science education.

Digital video and the construction of knowledge

Digital video serves as an invaluable resource and a compelling means for learning about teaching. The activities arising from its use bear the features of social constructivism as outlined by Hodson and Hodson (1998). Video-based activities can:

- » identify the views and needs of learners;
- » provide opportunities for learners to explore and test their current ideas;
- » provide stimuli and support for learners to revise or develop their thinking.

Conceptual change only occurs in the learner when they understand and appreciate the flaws and weaknesses in their current thinking (Posner et al, 1982). For new ideas to be assimilated into working knowledge, they must be '*intelligible*', '*plausible*' and '*fruitful*' (p 213). It is here that the value of video as a learning resource becomes evident. Repeating, pausing and annotating classroom footage make it more understandable and allow the experience to be aligned with other sources of knowledge, such as written texts or other video clips. Situating the concept within footage of the actual practice displays it as being both plausible and effective.

Digital video, with its associated activity and artefacts, can act as a scaffold to PSTs' learning. The features of a scaffold identified by Bruner (1997) are all provided by digital video (see Table 7.1).

Table 7.1 How video use bears the features of a scaffold as characterised by Bruner (1997)

Bruner's (1997) features of scaffolding	**Role of digital video**
Protect the learner from distraction by highlighting the significant feature of the problem.	Video editing and annotating can help structure observation tasks.
Sequence the steps to understanding.	Video clips can be selected, edited and sequenced to exemplify and enrich the narrative of instruction.
Enable negotiation.	Dialogue with tutors and peers, both in person and online, can access, challenge and progress thinking.
Know just what it is that the learner needs in order to succeed.	Video can identify specific skills to develop, and repeated cycles of practice can evidence progress.

Bruner (1997, p 68) points out that Vygotsky considered that meaning making requires not only language but also '*a grasp of the culture in which language is used*'. It also requires sustained social exchange through which higher orders of thinking '*gradually spread to the older concepts*' to produce new structures of knowledge. Vygotsky proposed that learning is most valuable when it takes place just ahead of development and that it requires a form of scaffolding or support to mediate this journey across the 'zone of proximal development'

(ZPD). Warford (2011, p 252) describes the ZPD as '*the distance between what a learner is able to do and a proximal level that they might attain through the guidance of an expert-other*'. Murphy and Scantlebury (2011), however, caution against a simplistic conceptualisation of the ZPD as a 'gap', which can be crossed with expert assistance, as is often the case within educational contexts. They cite Palinscar's (1998) view that too strong an emphasis has been given to the 'expert' nature of the other and insufficient emphasis has been placed on the importance of peer co-constitution of knowledge (Roth and Radford, 2010). The form of collaboration nurtured by video is closer to '*participatory appropriation*' than '*cognitive apprenticeship*' (Rogoff et al, 1993) as teachers '*stretch their common understanding to fit with new perspectives in the shared endeavour. Such stretching to fit several views and to accomplish something together is development*' (p 153). Where development is supported by video, we can consider activity to be taking place in the video-supported zone of proximal development (VSZPD) (see Figure 7.1).

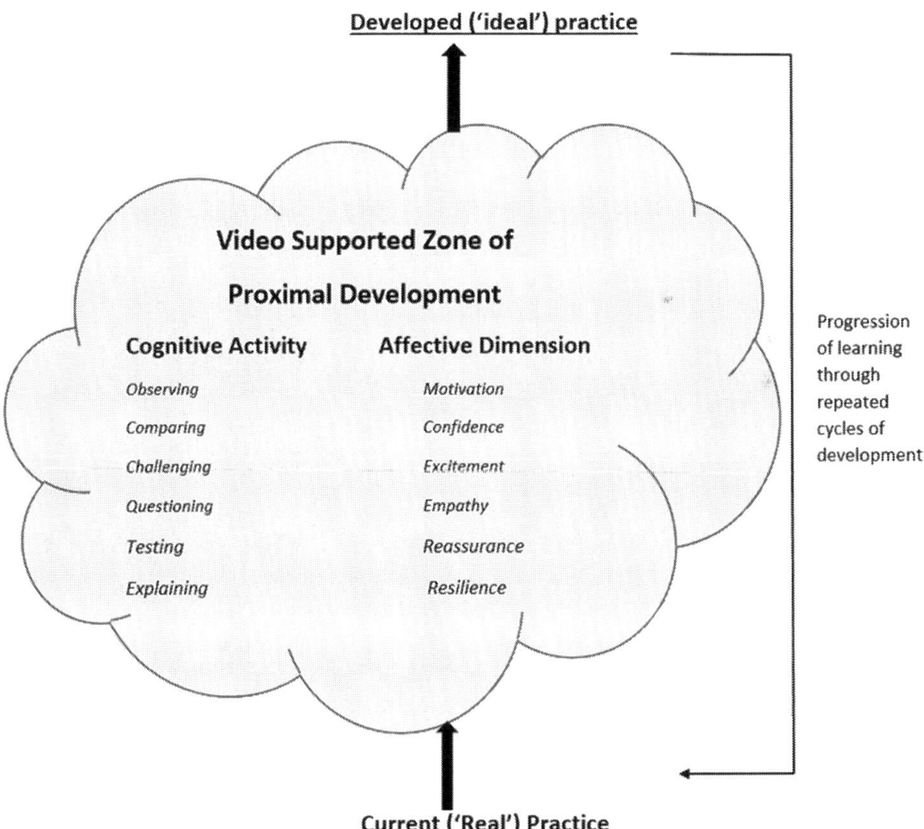

Figure 7.1 The relationship between the video supported zone of proximal development and pre-service teacher learning

The video-supported zone of proximal development

PSTs may be drawn into the VSZPD by their reaction to the experience of viewing video of themselves or others. This may invoke interest or curiosity in the practice of others or surprise at the sight and sound of their own teaching and so create a sense of dissatisfaction, relief or total shock. Within the VSZPD video plays a central role in initiating and enriching interaction and communication between PSTs and tutors. The VSZPD represents the conditions and activity which may support the PST in developing their current 'basic practice' to their 'ideal practice' with respect to a particular aspect of practice. Murphy and Scantlebury (2011) point out that Vygotsky considered emotion as an essential element of learning within the ZPD and that he used the word 'category' (which in Russian theatre referred to a dramatic event) to illustrate a high-impact social relation on the individual. The importance of the affective dimension to learning is addressed in their view (p 8) that '*a social relation which causes us to feel strongly, that is, a category, is more likely to be internalised and remembered, reflected on and lead to a change in behaviour*'. To be disappointed or shocked implies that the learner has a notion of what they think and would desire their practice to be like.

By observing others, in both real time and video recordings, the learners' initial notion of the ideal can be shifted and reconstructed. For their own practice, subsequent cycles of teaching and video recording can then be used to check for progress from dissonance to resonance, between current 'real' and developed 'ideal' practice. Digital video helps bring about dissatisfaction with current thinking, considered by Posner et al (1982) to be essential for learning, and presents a clear vision and path for development.

The VSZPD and the affective aspects of learning to teach

In addition to facilitating the cognitive activities of observing, comparing, challenging ideas, testing and questioning, the VSZPD attends to the emotional needs of the participants. Hobson et al's (2008) study of PSTs' experiences across a number of ITE programmes in England highlights the affective dimension to learning to teach. Many PSTs initially find being video recorded quite daunting and the analysis of self to be uncomfortable. However, the support of peers and feelings of collegiality and empathy with each other can sustain PSTs and make video analysis a rewarding experience. Hawkey (2006) claims that the role of emotion has been neglected within teacher education and that the stress of placement and the '*emotional whirlpool*' of starting to teach (Erb, 2002, p 235) may serve to inhibit cognitive learning. Hayes (2003) cautions that anxiety before placement can result in '*too much mental energy being directed towards concerns of the heart rather than the practical preparation for the job*'. While the support of peers is important, the reassurance resulting from watching a video of oneself teaching is also significant.

The value of the collaboration within the VSZPD is highlighted in Shepel's (1999, p 72) view that Dewey believed '*that the conceptual instruments of reflective thought are social human constructions ... and that the process of reflective thinking is deeply rooted in social interaction*'. Vygotsky also considered social-cultural influences to be fundamental in the formation and development of human thinking but paid less attention than Dewey to the societal processes. He claimed that for the individual, the social origin of higher levels of thinking lay with socially shared cognition between people (inter-psychological) and then with the individual themselves (intra-psychological). Vygotsky used the term 'internalisation' for this process by which social becomes psychological and considered language to play a key role. Hodson and Hodson (1998, p 36) suggest that '*language creates the possibility of thought, organises the thinking processes and both reflects and shapes the human society in which it is used*'. Granberg's (2010) study of PSTs' use of blogs within ITE also highlights the importance of peer dialogue. She takes Vygotsky's view that our inner speech is reduced when we are not required to explain or clarify our own thoughts to ourselves. She proposes that '*when we communicate our thoughts – both verbally or through written dialogue, we need to clarify our internal dialogue – both to our audience and to ourselves*' (p 348).

The role of self-efficacy beliefs in ITE

How can ITE programmes help ensure that PSTs' knowledge and understanding of practice lead to effective classroom teaching? Bandura (1982) cautions that a capability is only as good as its execution and that psychological theorising and research tend to focus on the acquisition of knowledge or the '*execution of response patterns*' (p 122) and neglect the interrelationship between knowledge and action. He points out that people do not always behave '*optimally*' even though they '*know full well what to do*' (p 122).

What PSTs believe regarding the effectiveness of their classroom practice is important, as it has a strong influence on how they perform. Efficacy is not simply a matter of knowing what to do but involves bringing cognitive, social and behavioural skills into action in order to deal with a particular classroom situation. Within teacher education, Tschannen-Moray et al (2001) describe self-efficacy belief (SEB) as a teacher's judgement of their capability to engage all pupils in learning. A teacher's level of SEB is important as it has a strong influence on how and what and they teach. Teachers with higher SEB are more likely to adopt more pupil-centred approaches to pedagogy (Sandholtz and Ringstaff, 2014), teach topics and subject areas they feel less confident in (Huinker and Madison, 1997) and are more open to exploring new forms of practice (Allinder, 1994). A person's SEB also influence how much energy they expend and how long they persist when confronted with problems and challenges (Bandura, 1982).

Doubts or misgivings about their ability to cope can divert PSTs' attention away from how best to proceed with a task to concerns over failing and mishaps. Concerns that they will be unable to cope with the demands of the classroom can be a source of anxiety among PSTs (Turner and Braine, 2016) and lead to stress. Resilience, or the capacity to bounce back in the face of setbacks, is also closely allied to self-efficacy (Gu and Day, 2007) and relies on PSTs '*knowing and believing in themselves*' (Turner and Braine, 2016, p 68).

How can video foster positive SEBs?

As there is evidence that SEBs can be increased (Palmer, 2011), their development should be included as a key objective of an ITE programme (d'Alessio, 2018). Bandura (1982) identified four sources of SEBs. Figure7.2 shows how each of these sources relates to the use of digital video within ITE.

Figure 7.2 How video can help develop PSTs' self-efficacy beliefs

Considered to have the greatest influence on the development of SEBs, *Enactive Mastery* represents activities which provide the learner with the knowledge and strategies to enact effective behaviour. The activities described as 'representations of practice' (Chapter 1), such as microteaching or planning tasks based on videos of exemplar lessons, help move PSTs towards 'mastery'. Repeated 'performance accomplishment' (d'Alessio, 2018) enhances SEB, while the experience of continuous failure will erode it. Bandura (1982) notes that failure can be particularly damaging when it comes early in the learning journey and despite no lack of effort on the part of the learner. Video can help build PSTs' SEB from the beginning of their studies both in and away from the classroom.

Watching video recordings of peers and taking part in microteaching presents opportunities for *Vicarious Modelling.* Seeing others perform successfully can raise self-efficacy expectations in observers who feel that they too possess the capabilities to master comparable activities. The findings from each of the case studies described in previous chapters indicated that PSTs can learn a great deal from watching video recordings of their peers. Previous studies of microteaching (McCullagh and Murphy, 2015) report the majority of PSTs felt that they learned as much about teaching from watching their peers' teaching, both live and on video, as they did from watching recordings of themselves. Peer feedback has been shown to provide cognitive support during microteaching (McCullagh and Doherty, 2018) and during periods of classroom teaching (Hayes, 2003; Hurley and Cammack, 2014). Video ensures that *Verbal Persuasion* is backed up by evidence and is therefore more convincing. Finally, confronting one's own practice in the form of a video provides *Emotional Arousal* and acts as a reality check.

Video as a means for 'learning in and from practice'

So far this book has described how digital video can help prepare PSTs for school placement and enable them to make the most of the learning opportunities it presents. The school placement element forms the cornerstone of all ITE programmes and therefore has been the subject of much discussion and the focus for calls to reform or adapt programmes in line with current policy and thinking across the world. The United States of America's National Council for Accreditation of Teacher Education's (2010, p 3) call to '*place practice at the centre of teacher preparation*', and Hiebert et al (2007) propose that PSTs learn how to teach from actually teaching and working through a clearly defined analysis framework to explore how their actions may support or restrict pupil learning. In parts of the UK the proportion of time PSTs spend in school has been increased by both legislation and the growth of school-centred models. Although government policy on ITE is more closely aligned with political ideologies and government budgetary considerations than it is guided by evidence of efficacy, it could be taken to suggest that being in school and teaching in classrooms best prepares PSTs (Murray and Mutton, 2016) and may even suggest a rejection of theory in favour of practice (Burn and Mutton, 2015). However, when it comes to learning from school experience '*more is not necessarily better*' (Kenny, 2010, p 1268). The assumption that pre-service teachers learn from school placements and that this experience '*melds theory into practice*' is challenged by Santagata et al (2007, p 124) who cautions that unstructured classroom observation can prove ineffectual and poorly planned school placements can '*expose students to a limited repertoire of strategies and to a narrow and unrepresentative sample of students*'.

McNamara (2013) research on workplace learning sets the bar high regarding the role of accommodating schools. They should provide high-quality learning activities within a communal learning culture in which student teachers are valued and in which '*symbiotic relationships between the multiple discourses about theory and practice, teaching and learning can be facilitated*'. Murray and Mutton (2016, p 9) contend that this binary conceptualisation of theory/practice and the related ITE institution/school divide is unhelpful, '*positioning schools as the only places where "practice" can be generated and universities as the sole "providers" of "theory", which is often viewed as irrelevant*'. An alternative view shifts the conceptualisation of teacher education from 'learning *for* practice' to 'learning *in and from* practice' (Ball and Cohen, 1999, p 5).

How might digital video inform the ITE structure and practices?

The need for more research into what constitutes an effective ITE has been made frequently (Hiebert et al, 2007; Darling-Hammond, 2010; Burn and Mutton, 2015; Philpott, 2014; Carter, 2015; Tatto and Furlong, 2015; Menter, 2016). The use of digital video so far described in this book speaks not only to how it is used within ITE but also to the key principles around which ITE programmes should be structured. From their study of effective ITE programmes, Korthagen et al (2006) identified seven 'fundamental principles' across the following three key components.

1. Views of knowledge and learning – something which is created.
2. Program structures and practices – centred on classroom practice which is collaborative and exploratory.
3. Quality of staff and organisation – strong partnership between ITE institutions and schools.

Their prescription is consistent with Darling-Hammond's (2006, p 1) view that twenty-first-century ITE programmes should prioritise '*extensive and intensely supervised clinical work integrated with coursework using pedagogies linking theory and practice, and closer, proactive relationships with schools*'.

Menter (2015) also identifies the 'relationship between theory and practice', and 'the sites of professional learning', as two of the six enduring themes within teacher education which require greater research. Carter's (2015) review of teacher education in England recommends that PSTs have the opportunity to experience school as early as possible in the programme, work together in groups and understand the importance of observation and how to observe effectively. He also recommends (p 21) that:

effective programmes give careful consideration to how trainees' learning experiences are structured … and ensure effective integration between different types of knowledge and skills trainees need to draw on in order to develop their own teaching and don't privilege 'theory' or 'practice' but integrate them in an environment where trainees have access to the practical wisdom of experts and can engage in a process of enquiry, in an environment where they are able to trial techniques and strategies and evaluate the outcomes.

Video as a third space for ITE

Video could be considered to provide a 'third space' in which PSTs can learn about teaching. Greca (2016) conceptualises a 'third space' as an arena where PSTs can discuss and explore their understanding and experience of teaching. The third space in Greca's (2016) study involves the online sharing and critiquing of PSTs' accounts of their practice

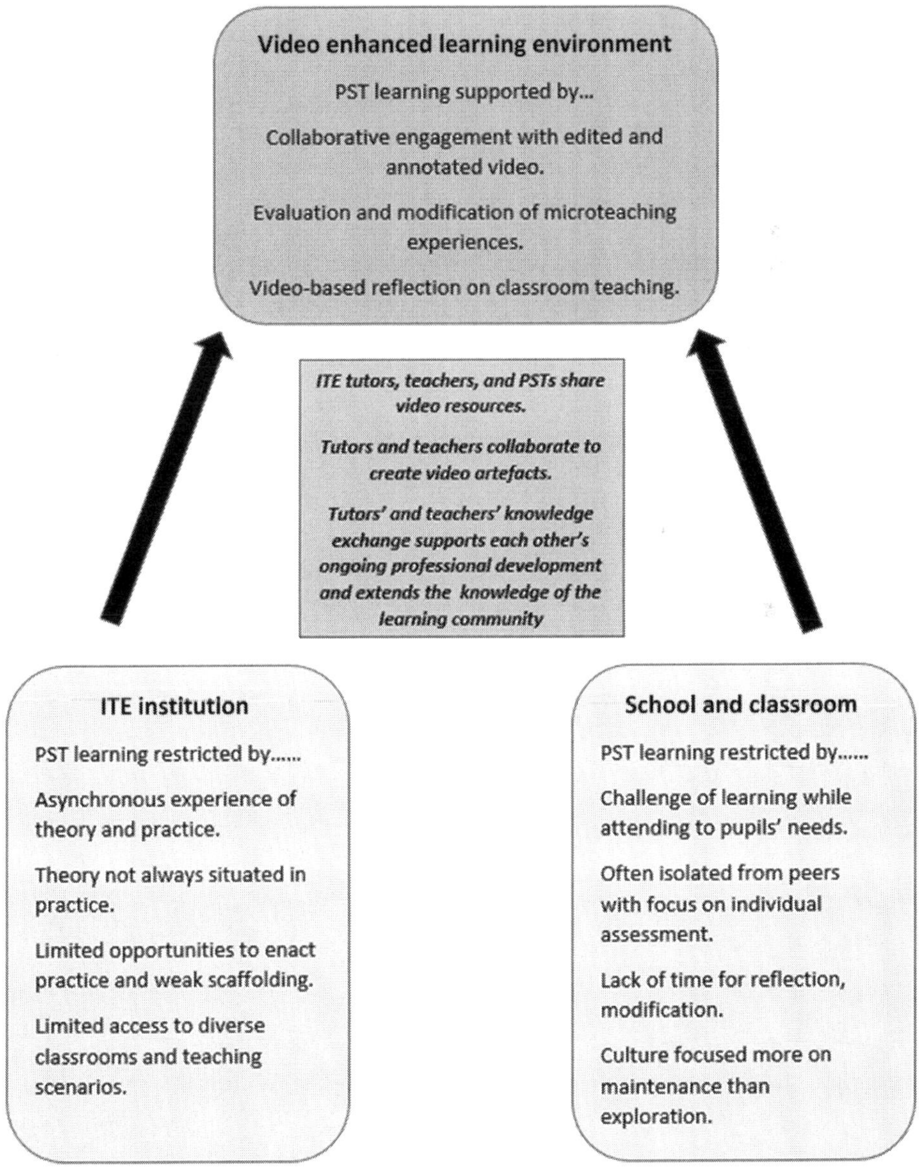

Figure 7.3 ITE and schools collaborate to create a video enhanced learning environment

and theory-informed perspectives on the teaching of science through inquiry. The premise of this space is that acknowledging and characterising the different forms of knowledge and experience acquired across the different phases and settings of their ITE programme can assist PSTs in bringing theory and practice closer together.

The shared use of video between ITE institutions and schools, tutors and cooperating teachers would allow for closer collaboration and constructive partnership between stakeholders. The third space could take the form of a video enhanced learning environment (VELE) containing videos, blogs and discussion forums which tutors, PSTs and teachers could contribute to and share (see Figure 7.3).

The VELE would serve as this third space in which PSTs could have access to the best of both worlds – the theory-rich discourse and pedagogical expertise of the ITE institution and the situated practice-related experience of in-service teachers. Videos could be jointly developed by both settings to support PSTs in planning and anticipating their classroom teaching. Including teachers in activities such as microteaching and video-based classroom management seminars would bring greater continuity to the PSTs' learning experience. It would, crucially, add considerable value to the quality and consistency of the supervision and support for PSTs throughout their placement in school. The stronger partnership would also help ITE tutors to keep up to date with current and innovative classroom pedagogy and in turn provide teachers and their schools with greater access to research-informed perspectives on practice.

IN A **NUTSHELL**

Digital video supports a form of ITE pedagogy consistent with a social constructivist view of learning. The technological and social affordances provided by video attend to the cognitive and affective needs of PSTs. The use of video can also enhance PSTs' SEB through enacting their own practice and observing and getting feedback from peers. Digital video could address some of the limiting features of current models of ITE provision by providing a video-supported learning space.

REFLECTIONS ON **CRITICAL ISSUES**

- *Digital video acts as a scaffold for learning by creating a video supported zone of proximal development.*
- *The activities arising from the use of digital video provide authentic opportunities for PSTs to develop their enactment of practice within a supportive and sharing culture.*
- *ITE provision could be enhanced by ITE institutions and their partner schools, collaborating to create and share digital videos and artefacts.*

References

Abell, S K and Cennamo, K S (2004) Videocases in Elementary Science Teacher Preparation, in J Brophy (ed) *Using Video in Teacher Education*. Oxford: Elsevier.

Akalin, S (2005) Comparison between Traditional Teaching and Microteaching during School Experience of Student-Teachers. *Eurasian Journal of Educational Research*, 20: 1–13.

Alger, C (2006) 'What Went Well. What Didn't Go so Well': Growth of Reflection in Pre-service Teachers. *Reflective Practice*, 7(3): 287–301.

Allen, D (1967) *Microteaching: A Description*. CA: U.S. Department of Health, Education and Welfare Office of Education.

Allinder, R M (1994) The Relationship between Efficacy and the Instructional Practices of Special Education Teachers and Consultants. *Teacher Education and Special Education*, 17(2): 86–95.

Amobi, F A (2005) Preservice Teachers' Reflectivity on the Sequence and Consequences of Teaching Actions in a Microteaching Experience. *Teacher Education Quarterly*, 32(1): 115–130.

Arsal, Z (2015) The Effects of Microteaching on the Critical Thinking Dispositions of Pre-service Teachers. *Australian Journal of Teacher Education*, 40(3): 140–153.

Baecher, L (2020) *Video in Teacher Learning: Through Their Own Eyes*. Thousand Oaks, CA: Corwin.

Baecher, L and Kung, S C (2011) Jumpstarting Novice Teachers' Ability to Analyze Classroom Video: Affordances of an Online Workshop. *Journal of Digital Learning in Teacher Education*, 28(1): 16–26.

Bahçivan, E (2017) Implementing Microteaching Lesson Study with a Group of Preservice Science Teachers: An Encouraging Attempt of Action Research. *International Online Journal of Educational Sciences*, 9(3): 591–603.

Bahcivan, E and Cobern, W W (2016) Investigating Coherence among Turkish Elementary Science Teachers' Teaching Belief Systems, Pedagogical Content Knowledge and Practice. *Australian Journal of Teacher Education*, 41(10): 62–86.

Baker, W D, Green, J L and Skukauskaite, A (2008) *Video-Enabled Ethnographic Research: A Microethnographic Perspective. How to Do Educational Ethnography*. London: Tufnell.

Ball, D and Forzani, F M (2009) The Work of Teaching and the Challenge for Teacher Education. *Journal of Teacher Education*, 60(5): 497–511.

Bambrick-Santoyo, P (2016) *Get Better Faster: A 90-Day Plan for Coaching New Teachers*. San Francisco, CA: Jossey-Bass.

Bandura, A (1982) Self-Efficacy Mechanism in Human Agency. *American Psychologist*, 37(2): 122–147.

Bell, N (2007) Microteaching: What Is Going on Here? *Linguistics and Education*, 18(1): 24–40.

Benton-Kupper,J (2001) The Microteaching Experience: Student Perspectives. *Education*, 121(4): 830–835.

Black, P and Wiliam, D (1998) Assessment and Classroom Learning. *Assessment in Education*, 5(1): 7–14.

Blomberg, G, Renkl, A, Sherin, M G, Borko, H and Seidel, T (2013) Five Research-Based Heuristics for Using Video in Pre-service Teacher Education. *Journal for Educational Research Online*, 5(1): 90–114.

Blomberg, G, Sherin, M G, Renkl, A, Glogger, I and Seidel, T (2014) Understanding Video as a Tool for Teacher Education: Investigating Instructional Strategies to Promote Reflection. *Instructional Science*, 42(3): 443–463.

Bolton, G (2010) *Reflective Practice: Writing and Professional Development*. 3rd ed. London: Sage.

Boud, D (2006) Relocating Reflection in the Context of Practice, in Bradbury, H, Frost, N, Kilminster, S and Zukas, M (eds) *Beyond Reflective Practice: New Approaches to Professional Lifelong Learning*. London: Routledge, pp 25–36.

Bousted, M, Hayes, D and Marshall, T (2011) What Do Teachers Want from Education? In D Hayes and T Marshall (eds) *In Defence of Teacher Education*. Worcester: Standing Committee for the Education and Training of Teachers (SCETT).

Brent, R, Wheatley, E and Thomson, W S (1996) Videotaped Microteaching: Bridging the Gap from the University to the Classroom. *The Teacher Educator*, 31(3): 238–247.

Brophy, J (ed) (2004a) *Advances in Research on Teaching: Using Video in Teacher Education* (Vol. 10). Oxford: Elsevier.

Brophy, J (ed) (2004b) *Using Video in Teacher Education*. Amsterdam: Elsevier.

Brouwer, C N (2011) *Imaging Teacher Learning. A Literature Review on the Use of Digital Video for Preservice Teacher Education and Professional Development*. Paper presented at the AERA Annual Meeting in New Orleans, April 11, 2011.

Brouwer, N (2015) Video-Based Reflection on Teaching: What Makes It Effective? *Orbis Scholae*, 9(2): 139–144.

Brouwer, N and Robijns, F (2015) In Search of Effective Guidance for Pre-service Teachers' Viewing of Classroom Videos, in B Calandra and P Rich (eds) *Digital Video for Teacher Education*. New York and London: Routledge.

Brown, J S and Duguid, P (1991) Organizational Learning and Communities-of-Practice: Toward a Unified View of Working, Learning, and Innovation. *Organization Science*, 2(1): 40–57.

Bruner, J (1997) Celebrating Divergence: Piaget and Vygotsky. *Human Development*, 40(2): 63–73.

Burn, K, Hagger, H and Mutton, T. (2015) *Beginning Teachers' Learning: Making Experience Count*. Plymouth: Critical Publishing.

Burn, K and Mutton, T (2015) A Review of 'Research-Informed Clinical Practice' in Initial Teacher Education. *Oxford Review of Education*, 41(2): 217–233.

Calandra, B (2015) A Process of Guided Video-Based Reflection, Chapter 3 in B Calandra and P Rich (eds) *Digital Video for Teacher Education*. New York and London: Routledge.

Calandra, B and Rich, P J (2015) *Digital Video for Teacher Education: Research and Practice*. New York and London: Routledge.

Calandra, B, Sun, Y and Puvirajah, A (2014) A New Perspective on Preservice Teachers' Video-Aided Reflection. *Journal of Digital Learning in Teacher Education*, 30(3): 104–109.

Canning, C (1991) What Teachers Say about Reflection. *Educational Leadership*, 48(6): 18–21.

Carter, A (2015) *Carter Review of Initial Teacher Training*. London: Department for Education. Available at: www.gov.uk/ government/uploads/system/uploads/attachment_data/file/399957/Carter_Review.pdf (accessed 18 June 2021)

Cattaneo, K H (2017) Telling Active Learning Pedagogies Apart: From Theory to Practice. *Journal of New Approaches in Educational Research*, 6(2): 144–152.

Chak, A (2006) Reflecting on the Self: An Experience in a Preschool. *Reflective Practice*, 7(1): 31–41.

Clarke, A (1995) Professional Development in Practicum Settings: Reflective Practice under Scrutiny. *Teaching and Teacher Education*, 11(3): 243–261.

Copeland, W D, Birmingham, C, de la Cruz, E and Lewin, B (1993) The Reflective Practitioner in Teaching: Toward a Research Agenda. *Teaching and Teacher Education*, 9(4): 347–359.

Crichton, H and Gil, F V (2015) Professional Partnership between Universities and Schools: the Use of a Diagnostic Tool to support Development of Student Teachers' Professional Skills. *Teacher Education Advancement Network Journal*, 7(1): 14–24.

Cruikshank, D and Metcalf, K (1993) Improving Pre-service Teacher Assessment through On-Campus Laboratory Experiences. *Theory into Practice*, 32(2): 86–92.

d'Alessio, M A (2018) The Effect of Microteaching on Science Teaching Self-Efficacy Beliefs in Preservice Elementary Teachers. *Journal of Science Teacher Education*, 29(6): 441–467.

Darling-Hammond, L (2006) Constructing 21st Century Teacher Education. *Journal of Teacher Education*, 57(3): 300–314.

Darling-Hammond, L (2010) Teacher Education and the American Future. *Journal of Teacher Education*, 61(1–2): 35–47.

Darling-Hammond, L, Hammerness, K, Grossman, P, Rust, F and Schulman, L (2007) The Design of Teacher Education Programs, in Darling-Hammond, L and Bransford, J (eds) *Preparing Teachers for a Changing World: What Teachers Should Learn and Be Able to Do.* San Francisco, CA: Jossey-Bass.

Davis, E A (2003) Prompting Middle School Science Students for Productive Reflection: Generic and Directed Prompts. *The Journal of the Learning Sciences*, 12(1): 91–142.

Deci, E and Ryan, R (1985) *Intrinsic Motivation and Self-Determination in Human Behaviour.* London: Plenum Press.

Dewey, J (1916) *Democracy and Education; An Introduction to the Philosophy of Education.* New York: Macmillan.

Dewey, J (1933) *How We Think.* Buffalo, NY: Prometheus Books.

Digby, R (2017) Video Stimulated Reflective Dialogue. *Journal of Emergent Science*, 12: 7–15.

Drew, V and Mackie, L (2011) Extending the Constructs of Active Learning: Implications for Teachers' Pedagogy and Practice, *The Curriculum Journal*, 22(4): 451–467.

Dyment, J and O'Connell, T S (2011) Assessing the Quality of Reflection in Student Journals: A Review of the Research. *Teaching in Higher Education*, 16(1): 81–97.

Eilam, B and Poyas, Y (2009) Learning to Teach: Enhancing Pre-service Teachers' Awareness of Complexity of Teaching-Learning Processes. *Teachers and Teaching*, 15(1): 87–107.

Endacott, J L (2016) Using Video-Stimulated Recall to Enhance Preservice-Teacher Reflection. *The New Educator*, 12(1): 28–47.

Eraut, M (2000) Non-formal Learning and Tacit Knowledge in Professional Work. *British Journal of Educational Psychology*, 70(1): 113–136.

Erb, C S (2002) *The Emotional Whirlpool of Beginning Teachers' Work.* In Annual Meeting of the Canadian Society of Studies in Education, Toronto, Canada.

Erickson, F (2007) Ways of Seeing Video: Toward a Phenomenology of Viewing Minimally Edited Footage, in Goldman, R, Pea, R, Barron, B and Derry, S (eds) *Video Research in the Learning Sciences.* NJ: Lawrence Erlbaum Associates.

Fadde, P J and Zhou, T (2015) Technical Considerations and Issues in Recording and Producing Classroom Video, in B Calandra and P Rich (eds) *Digital Video for Teacher Education.* New York and London: Routledge.

Feiman-Nemser, S (2001) From Preparation to Practice. Designing a Continuum to Strengthen and Sustain Teaching. *Teachers College Record*, 103(6): 1013–1053.

Fernandez, M L (2010) Investigating How and What Prospective Teachers Learn through Microteaching Lesson Study. *Teaching and Teacher Education*, 26(2): 351–362.

Fernsten, L and Fernsten, J (2005) Portfolio Assessment and Reflection: Enhancing Learning through Reflective Practice. *Reflective Practice*, 6(2): 303–309.

Fishman, B (2007) Fostering Community Knowledge, in Goldman, R, Pea, R, Barron, B and Derry, S J (eds) *Video Research in the Learning Sciences*. Mahwah, NJ: Lawrence Erlbaum.

Freire, P (1993) *Pedagogy of the Oppressed*. New York: Continuum Books.

Gardner, J and McNally, H (1995) Supporting School-Based Initial Teacher Training with Interactive Video. *British Journal of Educational Technology*, 26: 30–41.

Gibbons, S and Farley, A N (2019) The Use of Video Reflection for Teacher Education and Professional Learning. *Mid-Western Educational Researcher*, 31(2): 263–273.

Gibbs, G (1988) *Learning by Doing: A Guide to Teaching and Learning Methods*. Oxford: Further Education Unit.

Gleaves, A, Walker, C and Grey, J (2008) Using Digital and Paper Diaries for Assessment and Learning Purposes in Higher Education: A Case of Critical Reflection or Constrained Compliance? *Assessment & Evaluation in Higher Education*, 33(3): 219–231.

Goldman, R (2007a) ORION, An Online Digital Analysis Tool: Changing Our Perspectives as an Interpretive Community, in Goldman, R, Pea, R, Barron, B and Derry, S J (eds) *Video Research in the Learning Sciences*. Mahwah, NJ: Lawrence Erlbaum.

Goldman, R (2007b) Video Representations and the Perspectivity Frameworks: Epistemology, Ethnography, Evaluation, and Ethics, in Goldman, R, Pea, R, Barron, B and Derry, S J (eds) *Video Research in the Learning Sciences*. Mahwah, NJ: Lawrence Erlbaum.

Goldsmith, L T and Seago, N (2011) Using Classroom Artefacts to Focus Teachers' Noticing, in M Sherin, V Jacobs and R Phillipp (eds) *Mathematics Teacher Noticing: Seeing through Teachers' Eyes*. New York: Routledge.

Goodman, J (1988) Constructing a Practical Philosophy of Teaching: A Study of Preservice Teachers' Professional Perspectives. *Teaching and Teacher Education*, 4(2): 121–137.

Goodnough, K, Falkenberg, T and MacDonald, R (2016) Examining the Nature of Theory-Practice Relationships in Initial Teacher Education: A Canadian Case Study. *Canadian Journal of Education*, 39(1): 1–28.

Goodwin, C (1994) Professional Vision. *American Anthropologist*, 96(3): 606–633.

Gore, J M and Zeichner, K M (1991) Action Research and Reflective Teaching in Preservice Teacher Education: A Case Study from the United States. *Teaching and Teacher Education*, 7(2): 119–136.

Granberg, C (2010) Social Software for Reflective Dialogue: Questions about Reflection and Dialogue in Student Teachers' Blogs. *Technology, Pedagogy and Education*, 19(3): 345–360.

Greca, I M (2016) Supporting Pre-service Elementary Teachers in Their Understanding of Inquiry Teaching through the Construction of a Third Discursive Space. *International Journal of Science Education*, 38(5): 791–813.

Grossman, P, Compton, C, Igra, D, Ronfeldt, M, Shahan, E and Williamson, P (2009) Teaching Practice: A Cross-Professional Perspective. *Teachers College Record*, 111(9): 2055–2100.

Grossman, P and McDonald, M (2008) Back to the Future: Directions for Research in Teaching and Teacher Education. *American Educational Research Journal*, 45(1): 184–205.

GTCNI (2007) *Teaching: The Reflective Profession*. Belfast: GTCNI.

Gu, Q and Day, C (2007) Teachers' Resilience: A Necessary Condition for Effectiveness. *Teaching and Teacher Education*, 23(8): 1302–1316.

Hamachek, D (1995) *Psychology in Teaching, Learning, and Growth*. Boston, MA: Allyn and Bacon.

Harford, J and MacRuairc, G (2008) Engaging Student Teachers in Meaningful Reflective Practice. *Teaching and Teacher Education*, 24(7): 1884–1892.

Hatton, N and Smith, D (1995) Reflection in Teacher Education: Towards Definition and Implementation. *Teaching and Teacher Education*, 11(1): 33–49.

Hawkey, K (2006) Emotional Intelligence and Mentoring in Pre-service Teacher Education: A Literature Review. *Mentoring & Tutoring*, 14(2): 137–147.

Hayes, D (2003) Emotional Preparation for Teaching: A Case Study about Trainee Teachers in England. *Teacher Development*, 7(2): 153–171.

Hiebert, J, Gallimore, R and Stigler, J W (2002) A Knowledge Base for the Teaching Profession: What Would It Look Like and How Can We Get One? *Educational Researcher*, 31(5): 3–15.

Hiebert, J, Morris, A K, Berk, D and Jansen, A (2007) Preparing Teachers to Learn from Teaching. *Journal of Teacher Education*, 58(1): 47–61.

Higgins, R, Hartley, P and Skelton, A (2001) Getting the Message across: The Problem of Communicating Assessment Feedback. *Teaching in Higher Education*, 6(2): 269–274.

Hoath, L (2012) The Emotions of Reflective Practice. *Primary Science*, 125: 21–23.

Hobbs, V (2007) Faking It or Hating It: Can Reflective Practice Be Forced? *Reflective Practice*, 8(3): 405–417.

Hodson, D and Hodson, J (1998) From Constructivism to Social Constructivism: A Vygotskian Perspective on Teaching and Learning Science. *School Science Review*, 79(289): 33–41.

Huinker, D and Madison, S K (1997) Preparing Efficacious Elementary Teachers in Science and Mathematics: The Influence of Methods Courses. *Journal of Science Teacher Education*, 8(2): 107–126.

Hurley, A and Cammack, P (2014) 'Get a Backbone... Come On!' The Place of Emotional Intelligence in Pre-placement Preparation and Support for Trainee Teachers. *Teacher Education Advancement Network (TEAN) Journal*, 6(2): 13–24.

Husu, J, Toom, A and Patrikainen, S (2008) Guided Reflection as a Means to Demonstrate and Develop Student Teachers' Reflective Competencies. *Reflective Practice*, 9(1): 37–51.

I'Anson, J, Rodrigues, S and Wilson, G (2003) Mirrors, Reflections and Refractions: The Contribution of Microteaching to Reflective Practice. *European Journal of Teacher Education*, 26(2): 189–199.

Kellogg, R (1994) *The Psychology of Writing*. New York: Oxford University Press.

Kenny, J (2010) Preparing Pre-service Primary Teachers to Teach Primary Science: A Partnership-Based Approach. *International Journal of Science Education*, 32(10): 1267–1288.

Kerin, M (2019) *Coteaching Music in a Primary School: Teacher Perspectives*. PhD thesis. Trinity College Dublin.

Kilic, A (2010) Learner-Centered Micro Teaching in Teacher Education. *Online Submission*, 3(1): 77–100.

Klinzing, G and Floden, R E (1991) *The Development of the Microteaching Movement in Europe*. Paper presented at the Annual Meeting of the American Educational Research Association, Chicago, IL, April 3–7.

Kolb, D A (1984) *Experiential Learning: Experience as the Source of Learning and Development*. Englewood Cliffs, NJ: Prentice-Hall.

Korthagen, F and Kessels, J (1999) Linking Theory and Practice: Changing the Pedagogy of Teacher Education. *Educational Researcher*, 28(4): 4–17.

Korthagen, F, Kessels, J, Koster, B, Lagerwerf, B and Wubbels, T (2001) *Linking Practice and Theory: The Pedagogy of Realistic Teacher Education*. Mahwah, NJ: Lawrence Erlbaum Associates.

Korthagen, F, Loughran, J and Russell, T (2006) Developing Fundamental Principles for Teacher Education Programs and Practice. *Teaching and Teacher Education*, 22: 1020–1041.

Korthagen, F and Vasalos, A (2005) Levels in Reflection: Core Reflection as a Means to Enhance Professional Growth. *Teachers and Teaching*, 11: 47–71.

Kuswandono, P (2014) University Mentors' Views on Reflective Practice in Microteaching: Building Trust and Genuine Feedback. *Reflective Practice*, 15(6): 701–717.

Larrivee, B (2008) Development of a Tool to Assess Teachers' Level of Reflective Practice. *Reflective Practice*, 9(3): 341–360.

Lave, J and Wenger, E (1990) *Situated Learning: Legitimate Peripheral Participation*. Cambridge, UK: Cambridge University Press.

Le Fevre, D M (2004) *Designing for Teacher Learning: Video-Based Curriculum Design, Learning Sciences*. Mahwah, NJ: Lawrence Erlbaum.

Lee, H (2005) Understanding and Assessing Preservice Teachers' Reflective Thinking. *Teaching and Teacher Education*, 21: 699–715.

Lee, S K F and Loughran, J J (2000) Facilitating Pre-service Teachers' Reflection through a School-Based Teaching Programme. *Reflective Practice*, 1(1): 69–89.

Lofthouse, R. and Birmingham, P (2010) The Camera in the Classroom: Video-Recording as a Tool for Professional Development of Student Teachers. *Teacher Education Advancement Network (TEAN) Journal*, 1(2): 2–18.

Lortie, D (1975) *Schoolteacher: A Sociological Study*. Chicago, IL: University of Chicago Press.

Loughran, J J (2002) In Search of Meaning in Learning about Teaching. *Journal of Teacher Education*, 53(1): 33–43.

Luehmann, A L (2007) Identity as a Lens to Science Teacher Preparation. *Science Education*, 91: 822–839.

Luft, J A (2001) Changing Inquiry Practice and Beliefs: The Impact of an Enquiry-Based Professional Development Programme on Beginning and Experienced Secondary Science Teachers. *International Science Education*, 23(5): 517–534.

Lundeberg, M A and Scheurman, G (1997) Looking Twice Means Seeing More: Developing Pedagogical Knowledge through Case Analysis. *Teaching and Teacher Education*, 13(8): 783–797.

Marsh, B and Mitchell, N (2014) The Role of Video in Teacher Professional Development. *Teacher Development*, 18(3): 403–417.

Martin, S N and Siry, C (2012) Using Video in Science Teacher Education: An Analysis of the Utilization of Video-Based Media by Teacher Educators and Researchers, in B Fraser, K Tobin and C McRobbie (eds) *Second International Handbook of Science Education*. Dordrecht: Springer.

Mason, J (2002) *Researching Your Own Practice: The Discipline of Noticing*. New York and London: Routledge.

Mason, J (2011) Noticing: Roots and Branches, in Sherin, M G, Jacobs, V R and Philipp, R A (eds) *Mathematics Teacher Noticing: Seeing through Teachers' Eyes*. New York and London: Routledge.

McCullagh, J F and Doherty, A (2018) Digital Makeover: What Do Pre-service Teachers Learn from Microteaching Primary Science and How Does an Online Video Analysis Tool Enhance this Activity? *Teacher Education Advancement Journal (TEAN)*, 10(2): 15–28.

McCullagh, J F and Murphy, C (2015) *From Microteaching to Microlearning: The Final Report on the Video in STEM Teacher Assessment (VISTA) Project*. Belfast: Stranmillis University, SCoTENS.

McDonald, M, Kazemi, E and Kavanagh, S S (2013) Core Practices and Pedagogies of Teacher Education: A Call for a Common Language and Collective Activity. *Journal of Teacher Education*, 64(5): 378–386.

McDonald, S and Rook, M M (2015) Digital Video Analysis to Support the Development of Professional Pedagogical Vision, in B Calandra and P Rich (eds) *Digital Video for Teacher Education*. New York and Abingdon: Routledge.

McFadden, J, Ellis, J, Anwar, T and Roehrig, G (2014) Beginning Science Teachers' Use of a Digital Video Annotation Tool to Promote Reflective Practices. *Journal of Science Education and Technology*, 23(3): 458–470.

McGarvey, B and Swallow, D. (1986) *Microteaching in Teacher Education and Training*. London: Croom Helm.

McIntyre, D, MacLeod, G and Griffiths, R (1977) *Investigations of Microteaching*. London: Croom Helm.

McNamara, J (2013) The Challenge of Assessing Professional Competence in Work Integrated Learning. *Assessment and Evaluation in Higher Education*, 38(2): 183–197.

McNamara, O, Murray, J and Jones, M (2014) Workplace Learning in Pre-service Teacher Education: An English Case Study, in McNamara, O, Murray, J and Jones M (eds) *Professional Learning and Development in Schools and Higher Education Volume 10*. New York: Springer.

Menter, I (2015) Teacher Education, in J D Wright (ed) *International Encyclopedia of the Social & Behavioral Sciences*. 2nd ed. Vol 24. Oxford: Elsevier.

Menter, I (2016) What Is a Teacher in the 21st Century and What Does a 21st Century Teacher Need to Know? *Acta Didactica Norge*, 10(2): 11–25.

Metcalf, K K, Hammer, M R and Kahlich, P A (1996) Alternatives to Field-Based Experiences: The Comparative Effects of On-Campus Laboratories. *Teaching and Teacher Education*, 12(3): 271–283.

Mewborn, D and Tyminski, A (2006) Lortie's Apprenticeship of Observation Revisited. *For the Learning of Mathematics*, 26(3): 30–32.

Michael, J (2006) Where's the Evidence that Active Learning Works? *Advance in Physiology Education*, 30: 159–167.

Morris, A K (2007) Assessing Pre-service Teachers' Skills for Analysing Teaching. *Journal of Mathematics Teacher Education*, 58(1): 47–61.

Morrison, B (2010) Teacher Training in China and the Role of Teaching Practice. [online] Available at: http://sunzil.lib.hku.hk/hkj/view/45/4500089/pdf

Murphy, C (2016) *Coteaching in Teacher Education: Innovative Pedagogy for Excellence*. St Albans: Critical Publishing.

Murphy, C and Scantlebury, K (2011) *Coteaching in Science and Mathematics: A Vygotskian Framework for Enhancing Teacher Professional Development to Effect Classroom Transformation*. National Association of Research on Science Teaching (NARST) Annual Conference Orlando, April 2011.

Murray, J and Mutton, T (2016) Teacher Education in England: Change in Abundance, Continuities in Question, in *Teacher Education in Times of Change*. Bristol: Policy Press, pp 57–74.

Nahavandi, A (2006) Teaching Leadership to First Year Students in a Learning Community. *Journal of Leadership Education*, 5(2): 12–27.

Napoles, J (2008) Relationships among Instructor, Peer, and Self-Evaluations of Undergraduate Music Education Majors' Micro-Teaching Experiences. *Journal of Research in Music Education*, 56(1): 82–91.

Ng, P T and Tan, C (2009) Community of Practice for Teachers: Sensemaking or Critical Reflective Learning? *Reflective Practice*, 10(1): 37–44.

Nicol, D and Mac Farlane-Dick, D (2006) Formative Assessment and Self-Regulated Learning: A Model and Seven Principles of Good Feedback Practice. *Studies in Higher Education*, 31(2): 199–218.

Norman, G R and Schmidt, H G (1992) The Psychological Basis of Problem-Based Learning: A Review of the Evidence. *Academic Medicine*, 67(9): 557–565.

Olivero, J L (1965) *The Use of Video Recordings in Teacher Education*. Standford, CA: US Dept of Health, Education and Welfare.

Ottesen, E (2007) Reflection in Teacher Education. *Reflective Practice*, 8(1): 31–46.

Paivio, A (1990) *Mental Representations: A Dual Coding Approach*. Oxford: Oxford University Press.

Paley, V (1986) On Listening to What the Children Say. *Harvard Educational Review*, 56(2): 122–131.

Palincsar, A S (1998) Keeping the Metaphor of Scaffolding Fresh—A Response to C. Addison Stone's "The Metaphor of Scaffolding: Its Utility for the Field of Learning Disabilities". *Journal of Learning Disabilities*, 31(4): 370–373.

Papert, S and Harel, I (1991) *Constructionism*. Norwood, NJ: Ablex Publishing.

Parsons, M and Stephenson, M (2005) Developing Reflective Practice in Student Teachers: Collaboration and Critical Partnerships. *Teachers and Teaching*, 11(1): 95–116.

Pea, R D (1993) Practices of Distributed Intelligence and Design for Education, in G Salomon (ed) *Distributed Cognitions: Psychological and Educational Considerations*. New York: Cambridge University Press.

Pedro, J (2005) Reflection in Teacher Education: Exploring Pre-service Teachers' Meanings of Reflective Practice. *Reflective Practice*, 6(1): 49–66.

Peker, M (2009) The Use of Expanded Microteaching for Reducing Pre-service Teachers' Teaching Anxiety about Mathematics. *Scientific Research and Essay*, 4(9): 872–880.

Pérez-Torregrosa, A B, Díaz-Martín, C and Ibáñez-Cubillas, P (2017) The Use of Video Annotation Tools in Teacher Training. *Procedia-Social and Behavioural Sciences*, 237: 458–464.

Philipp, R A, Ambrose, R, Lamb, L L, Sowder, J T, Schappelle, B P, Sowder, L, Thanheiser, E and Chauvot, J (2007) Effects of Early Field Experiences on the Mathematical Content Knowledge and Beliefs of Prospective Elementary School Teachers: An Experimental Study. *Journal for Research in Mathematics Education*, 38(5): 438–476.

Philpott, C (2014) A Pedagogy for Teacher Education in England. *Teacher Education Advancement Network Journal (TEAN)*, 6(3) Special Issue 2: 4–16.

Pollard, A (2019) *Reflective Teaching in Schools*. 5th ed. London: Bloomsbury Academic.

Posner, G J, Strike, K A, Hewson, P W and Gertzog, W A (1982) Accommodation of a Scientific Conception: Toward a Theory of Conceptual Change. *Science Education*, 66(2): 211–227.

Prince, M (2004) Does Active Learning Work? A Review of the Research. *Journal of Engineering Education*, 93(3): 223–231.

Rich, P J and Hannafin, M (2009) Video Annotation Tools Technologies to Scaffold, Structure, and Transform Teacher Reflection. *Journal of Teacher Education*, 60(1): 52–67.

Rich, P J and Trip, T (2011) Ten Essential Questions Educators Should Ask When Using Video Annotation Tools. *TechTrends*, 55(6): 16–24.

Richardson, V and Kile, R (1999) Learning from Videocases, in M A Lunderberg, B B Levin and H L Harrington (eds) *Who Learns What from Cases and How?: The Research Base for Teaching and Learning with Cases*.Mahwah, NJ: Lawrence Erlbaum Associates.

Rickard, A, McAvinia, C and Quirke-Bolt, N (2009) The Challenge of Change: Digital Video-Analysis and Constructivist Teaching Approaches on a One Year Preservice Teacher Education Program in Ireland. *Journal of Technology and Teacher Education*, 17(3): 349–367.

Roberts, C and Westville, I N (2008) Developing Future Leaders: The Role of Reflection in the Classroom. *Journal of Leadership Education*, 7(1): 116–130.

Rocco, S (2005) Making Reflection Public: Using Interactive Online Discussion Board to Enhance Student Learning. *Reflective Practice*, 11(3): 307–317.

Rodgers, C, Anderson, M, Burkett, B, Conley, S, Stanley, C and Turpin, L (2021) Reconstructing and Reorganizing Experience: Weaving a Living Philosophy. *Teachers College Record*, 123(6).

Rodgers, C and LaBoskey, V (2016) Reflective Practice, in J Loughran and M L Hamilton (eds) *International Handbook of Teacher Education*. Singapore: Springer

Rodgers, C R (2002a) Defining Reflection: Another Look at John Dewey and Reflective Thinking. *Teachers College Record*, 104(4): 842–866.

Rodgers, C R, (2002b) Seeing Student Learning: Teacher Change and the Role of Reflection. *Harvard Educational Review*, 72(2): 230–253.

Rogoff, B, Mistry, J, Göncü, A, Mosier, C, Chavajay, P and Heath, S B (1993) Guided Participation in Cultural Activity by Toddlers and Caregivers. *Monographs of the Society for Research in Child Development*, 58: i–179.

Rook, M M and McDonald, S (2012) Digital Records of Practice: A Literature Review of Video Analysis in Teacher Practice, in P Resta (ed) *Proceedings of Society for Information Technology & Teacher Education International Conference 2012.* Chesapeake, VA: AACE.

Rosaen, C L, Lundeberg, M, Cooper, M, Fritzen, A and Terpstra, M (2008) Noticing Noticing: How Does Investigation of Video Records Change How Teachers Reflect on Their Experiences? *Journal of Teacher Education*, 59(4): 347–360.

Roth, W (2007) Epistemic Mediation: Video Data as Filters for the Objectification of Teaching by Teachers, in R Goldman, R Pea, B Barron and S J Derry (eds) *Video Research in the Learning Sciences*. London: Lawrence Erlbaum Associates, pp 383–395.

Roth, W M and Radford, L (2010) Re/thinking the Zone of Proximal Development (Symmetrically). *Mind, Culture, and Activity*, 17(4): 299–307.

Sadler, D R (1989) Formative Assessment and the Design of Instructional Systems. *Instructional Science*, 18: 119–144.

Sadler, D R (1998) Formative Assessment: Revisiting the Territory. *Assessment in Education*, 5(1): 77–84.

Sandholtz, J H and Ringstaff, C (2014) Inspiring Instructional Change in Elementary School Science: The Relationship between Enhanced Self-Efficacy and Teacher Practices. *Journal of Science Teacher Education*, 25(6): 729–751.

Santagata, R and Angelici, G (2010) Studying the Impact of the Lesson Analysis Framework on Preservice Teachers' Ability to Reflect on Videos of Classroom Teaching. *Journal of Teacher Education*, 61(4): 339–349.

Santagata, R, Gallimore, R and Stigler, J W (2005) The Use of Videos for Teacher Education and Professional Development: Past Experiences and Future Directions, in C Vrasidas and G V Glass (eds) *Current Perspectives on Applied Information Technologies: Preparing Teachers to Teach with Technology*. Greenwich, CT: Information Age Publishing.

Santagata, R and Guarino, J (2011) Using Video to Teach Future Teachers to Learn from Teaching. *ZDM Mathematics Education*, 43(1): 133–145.

Santagata, R, Zannoni, C and Stigler, J W (2007) The Role of Lesson Analysis in Pre-service Teacher Education: An Empirical Investigation of Teacher Learning from a Virtual Video-Based Field Experience. *Journal of Mathematics Teacher Education*, 10(2): 123–140.

Schön, D A (1983) *The Reflective Practitioner: How Professionals Think in Action*. New York: Basic Books.

Schulman, L S (1987) Knowledge and Teaching: Foundations of the New Reform. *Harvard Educational Review*, 57(1): 1–22.

Seidel, T, Stürmer, K, Blomberg, G, Kobarg, M and Schwindt, K (2011) Teacher Learning from Analysis of Videotaped Classroom Situations: Does It Make a Difference Whether Teachers Observe Their Own Teaching or that of Others? *Teaching and Teacher Education*, 27(2): 259–267.

Sellers, M (2017) *Reflective Practice for Teachers*. 2nd ed. London: Sage.

Shepel, E L (1999) Reflective Thinking in Educational Praxis: Analysis of Multiple Perspectives. *Educational Foundations*, 13: 69–88.

Sherin, M G (2004) New Perspectives on the Role of Video in Teacher Education, in J Brophy (ed) *Advances in Research on Teaching, Vol. 10, Using Video in Teacher Education*. Oxford: Elsevier, Ltd.

Sherin, M G (2007) Professional Vision, in R Goldman, R Pea, B Barron and S J Derry (eds) *Video Research in the Learning Sciences*. London: Lawrence Erlbaum Associates.

Sherin, M G and Russ, R S (2015) Teacher Noticing Via Video: The Role of Interpretative Frames, in B Calandra and P Rich (eds) *Digital Video in Teacher Education*. New York and Abingdon: Routledge, pp 3–20.

Sherin, M G and van Es, E (2005) Using Video to Support Teachers' Ability to Notice Classroom Interactions. *Journal of Technology and Teacher Education*, 13(3): 475–491.

Shwartz, D and Hartman, K (2007) It's not Television Anymore: Designing Digital Video for Learning and Assessment, in Goldman, R, Pea, R, Barron, B and Derry, S (eds) *Video Research in the Learning Sciences*. NJ: Lawrence Erlbaum Associates.

Sigel, I E (1993) The Centrality of a Distancing Model for the Development of Representational Competence, in R R Cocking and K A Renninger (eds) *The Development and Meaning of Psychological Distance*. New York: Psychology Press.

Siry, C and Martin, S N (2014) Facilitating Reflexivity in Preservice Science Teacher Education Using Video Analysis and Cogenerative Dialogue in Field-Based Methods Courses. *Eurasia Journal of Mathematics, Science & Technology Education*, 10(5): 481–508.

Smyth, J (1989) Developing and Sustaining Critical Reflection in Teacher Education. *Journal of Teacher Education*, 40(2): 2–9.

Snyder, K D (2003) Ropes, Poles, and Space: Active Learning in Business Education. *Active Learning in Higher Education*, 4(2): 159–167.

Spalding, E, Wilson, A and Mewborn, A (2002) Demystifying Reflection: A Study of Pedagogical Strategies that Encourage Reflective Journal Writing. *The Teachers College Record*, 104(7): 1393–1421.

Sparks-Langer, G M (1992) In the Eye of the Beholder: Cognitive, Critical, and Narrative Approaches to Teacher Reflection, in L Valli (ed) *Reflective Teacher Education: Cases and Critiques*. Albany, NY: State University of New Press, pp 147–160.

Spiro, R, Collins, B and Ramchandran, A (2007) Reflections on a Post-Guttenberg Epistemology for Video Use in Ill-Structured Domains: Fostering Complex Learning and Cognitive Flexibility, in Goldman, R, Pea, R, Barron, B and Derry, S (eds) *Video Research in the Learning Sciences*. NJ: Lawrence Erlbaum Associates.

Stanley, C (1998) A Framework for Teacher Reflectivity. *TESOL quarterly*, 32(3): 584–591.

Stapleton, J, Tschida, C and Cuthrell, K (2017) Partnering Principal and Teacher Candidates: Exploring a Virtual Coaching Model in Teacher Education. *Journal of Technology and Teacher Education*, 25(4): 495–519.

Stapleton, J, Tschida, C and Cuthrell, K (2017) Partnering Principal and Teacher Candidates: Exploring a Virtual Coaching Model in Teacher Education. *Journal of Technology and Teacher Education*, 25(4): 495–519.

Stetsenko, A (2008) From Relational Ontology to Transformative Activist Stance on Development and Learning. *Cultural Studies of Science Education*, 3(2): 471–491.

Stevens, R (2007) Capturing Ideas in Digital Things: A New Twist on the Old Problem of Inert Knowledge, in Goldman, R, Pea, R, Barron, B and Derry, S J (eds) *Video Research in the Learning Sciences*. Mahwah, NJ: Lawrence Erlbaum.

Stroupe, D and Gotwals, A W (2018) "It's 1000 Degrees in Here When I Teach": Providing Preservice Teachers with an Extended Opportunity to Approximate Ambitious Instruction. *Journal of Teacher Education*, 69(3): 294–306.

Subramaniam, K (2006) Creating a Microteaching Evaluation Form: The Needed Evaluation Criteria. *Education*, 126(4): 666–667.

Sweller, J (2010) Cognitive Load Theory: Recent Theoretical Advances, in J L Plass, R Moreno and R Brünken (eds) *Cognitive Load Theory*. Cambridge, UK: Cambridge University Press.

Taggart, G L and Wilson, A P (2005) *Promoting Reflective Thinking in Teachers: 50 Action Strategies*. 2nd ed. CA: Corwin Press.

Tatto, M T and Furlong, J (2015) Research and Teacher Education: Papers from the BERA-RSA Inquiry. *Oxford Review of Education*, 41(2): 145–153.

Tekkumru-Kisa, M and Stein, M K (2017) A Framework for Planning and Facilitating Video-Based Professional Development. *International Journal of STEM Education*, 4(1): 1–18.

Thom, J (2018) *Slow Teaching: On Finding Calm, Clarity and Impact in the Classroom*. Melton: John Catt Education Ltd.

Thomas, J A and Pedersen, J E (2003) Reforming Elementary Science Teacher Preparation: What about Extant Teaching Beliefs? *School Science and Mathematics*, 103(7): 319–330.

Tschannen-Moran, M and Hoy, A W (2001) Teacher Efficacy: Capturing an Elusive Construct. *Teaching and Teacher Education*, 17(7): 783–805.

Tschida, C M, Gallagher, J L, Anderson, K L, Ryan, C L, Stapleton, J N and Jones, K D (2019) Using Video Capture and Annotation Technology to Strengthen Reflective Practices and Feedback in Educator Preparation, in *Handbook of Research on Emerging Practices and Methods for K-12 Online and Blended Learning*. Hershey, PA: IGI Global.

Turner, S and Braine, M (2016) Embedding Wellbeing Knowledge and Practice into Teacher Education: Building Emotional Resilience. *Teacher Education Advancement Network Journal (TEAN)*, 8(1): 67–82.

Van Der Westhuizen, C P and Golightly, A (2015) Video Annotation Software Application for thorough Collaborative Assessment of and Feedback on Microteaching Lessons in Geography Education. *Journal of Geography in Higher Education*, 39(3): 420–436.

van Es, E, Tunney, J, Seago, N and Goldsmith L L (2015) Facilitation Practices for Supporting Teacher Learning with Video, in B Calandra and P Rich (eds) *Digital Video for Teacher Education*. New York and London: Routledge.

Van Manen, M (1977) Linking Ways of Knowing with Ways of Being Practical. *Curriculum Inquiry*, 6: 205–228.

Vygotsky, L S (2004) Thinking and Speech, in R Rieber and D Robbinson (eds) *Essential Vygotsky.* New York: Kluwer Academic/Plenum.

Ward, J R and McCotter, S S (2004) Reflection as a Visible Outcome for Preservice Teachers. *Teaching and Teacher Education*, 20(3): 243–257.

Warford, M K (2011) The Zone of Proximal Teacher Development. *Teaching and Teacher Education*, 27(2): 252–258.

Watkins, C, Carnell, E and Lodge, C (2007) *Effective Learning in Classrooms*. London: Sage.

Weber, K E, Gold, B, Prilop, C N and Kleinknecht, M (2018) Promoting Pre-service Teachers' Professional Vision of Classroom Management during Practical School Training: Effects of a Structured Online- and Video-Based Self-Reflection and Feedback Intervention. *Teaching and Teacher Education*, 76: 39–49.

Wertsch, J V (1997) *Vygotsky and the Formation of the Mind*. Cambridge, MA: Harvard University Press.

Whitehead, A (1929) *The Aims of Education and Other Essays*. New York: Macmillan.

Williams, J B, Bedi, K and Goldberg, M A (2006) The Impact of Digital Storytelling on Social Agency: Early Experience at an Online University. Available at: https://papers.ssrn.com/sol3/papers.cfm?abstract_id=1606104 (accessed April 2021)

Yadav, A and Koehler, M (2007) The Role of Epistemological Beliefs in Preservice Teachers' Interpretation of Video Cases of Early-Grade Literacy Instruction. *Journal of Technology and Teacher Education*, 15(3): 335–361.

Yalmanci, S Y and Aydin, S (2014) The Views of Turkish Pre-service Teachers Concerning Microteaching Practices. *Turkish Journal of Education*, 3(4): 4–14.

Yerrick, R, Thompson, M, MacDonald, S and McLaughlin, S (2011) Collected from the Cutting Room Floor: An Examination of Teacher Education Approaches to Digital Video Editing as a Tool for Shifting Classroom Practices. *Contemporary Issues in Technology and Teacher Education*, 11(1): 118–148.

Zeichner, K and Liston, D (1987) Teaching Student Teachers How to Reflect. *Harvard Educational Review*, 57: 23–48.

Zeichner, K (1983) Alternative Paradigms in Teacher Education. *Journal of Teacher Education*, 34(3): 3–9.

Zeichner, K (1996) Designing Educative Practicum Experiences, in Zeichner, K, Melnick, S and Gomez, M L (eds) *Currents of Reform in Pre-service Teacher Education*. New York: Teachers College Press.

Zhang, M, Lundeberg, M and Eberhardt, J (2010) Seeing What You Don't Normally See. *Phi Delta Kappan*, 91(6): 60–65.

Zhang, S and Cheng, Q (2011) Learning to Teach through a Practicum-Based Microteaching Model. *Action in Teacher Education*, 33(4): 343–358.

Zweck, J (2006) Strategies to Promote Active Learning in Math/Stat Discussion Sessions. Available at: http://www.math.umbc.edu/!zweck/TATrain/ActiveLearningStrategies.pdf.

Index

activating experience, 31
active learning, 35–36, 47
ALACT model, 59
Allen, Dwight, 13
Amobi, F A, 31, 56
'apprenticeship of observation,' 4
'approximate ambitious instruction,' 5
approximations of practice, 6–7

Baecher, L, 36, 37
Bandura, A, 77, 78
beginning repertoire, 44
being present, importance of, 60–61
Birmingham, P, 68
Blomberg, G, 9
Bolton, G, 31
Brouwer, C N, 38, 42, 43
Brown, J S, 20
Bruner, J, 74
  features of scaffolding, 74
Burn, K, 20

Calandra, B, 25
Carter, A, 80
Chak, A, 33
classroom observation
  and learning, 24–25
  professional vision, 25–26
  video-based introductory activity, 26
    case study, 26–28
classroom practice
  challenges of assessing, 63–64
    case study, 64–66
  digital video and
    formative assessment and feedback, 66–69
    summative assessment, 66
  high-quality feedback, learning from, 70
  microteaching impact on, 22
  role of tutor, 69
cognitive model of learning, 2
collectivist culture, 21
crowded curriculum, 50

Danielowich, R M, 69
Darling-Hammond, L, 63, 80
Davis, E A, 56
deconstruction of practice, 6–7
demand-style learning, 20
Derrida, J, 51
Dewey, J, 35, 36, 49, 56
  principles of reflection, 61
Digby, R, 21

digital video, 1, 2, 5, 11, 47, *see also individual entries*
  analysis tasks for PSTs, 36–37
    case study, 37–38
  change in post-lesson evaluations, 33
  and classroom practice
    formative assessment and feedback, 66–69
    to support summative assessment, 66
  and construction of knowledge, 73–75
  cycle of reflection, 59
  and distancing from 'self,' 33–34
  editing tasks, 46–47
  interaction with, 38–41
  ITE structure and practices, 80
  learning in and from practice, 79–80
  limitations of, 8–9
  and modelling of practice, 28
    case study, 28–30
  for objectification of self, 31
    case study, 31–33
  objectives of, 2
  pedagogies of practice, 6–7
  playback software, 8
  PSTs' reflections, enhancing quality of, 56–57
  recordings, 4
    commentary, 9
    hyperlinks, 8
    on-screen prompts, 9
    realness of, 11
  and skills development, 5
  technological and social affordances of, 72–73
  technology, 1, 11
  as third space for ITE, 81–82
  as tool for action, 73
  use in ITE, 2–5
discipline of description, 60
dual coding theory, 30
Duguid, P, 20

edited video content, 8
Eilam, B, 34
Emotional Arousal, 79
Enactive Mastery, 78
Eraut, M, 31
Erickson, F, 8

facilitators, 9
Fadde, P J, 8
Feiman-Nemser, S, 2, 4, 44
Fernsten, J, 50
Fernsten, L, 50
fine-grain analysis of practice, 4
Floden, R E, 12

Gardner, J, 8
General Teaching Council for Northern Ireland's competence model, 64
Gleaves, A, 50
Goodwin, C, 25
Gotwals, A W, 5, 73
Granberg, C, 77
Greca, I M, 80
Grossman, P, 6
Guarino, J, 30, 69

Hatton, N, 50
Hawkey, K, 76
Hayes, D, 76
Hiebert, J, 79
Hoath, L, 52
Hobbs, V, 50
Hobson, A, 76
Hodson, D, 73, 77
Hodson, J, 73, 77
human improvement, 6

initial teacher education (ITE), 1, *see also individual entries*
  digital video and, 2, 73, 80
  reflective practice and, 48–49
  self-efficacy beliefs in, 77
  video as third space for, 81–82
instructional triangle, 44
internalisation, 77
interpretative frames, 26, 27
ITE, *see* initial teacher education

Kilic, A, 20
Klinzing, G, 12
knowledge-based reasoning, 25, 34
Koehler, M, 31
Korthagen, F, 59, 80
Kuswandono, P, 21

LaBoskey, V, 56
Larivee, B, 50, 57
  levels of reflection, 57–58
learner-centred, 18, 19
  microteaching, 20
  problem-solving approach, 2
learning to teach, 11, 23
  challenges of, 5–6
  PSTs in, 3
  VSZPD and affective aspects of, 76–77
Lofthouse, R., 68
Lundeberg, M A, 26

MacFarlane-Dick, D, 66, 68
Marsh, B, 4
Martin, S N, 21
Mason, J, 24
McCarthy, J M, 69
McCotter, S S, 51
McDonald, M, 6
McGarvey, B, 22
McNally, H, 8
McNamara, J, 79
Menter, I, 80
microteaching, 12–13, 23
  benefits of, 13–14
  impact of, 22
  maximising learning from, 17
    case study, 18–19
    collaborative, 20–21
    learner-centred, 20
    product oriented, 21
  video supported learning within, 15
    case study, 15–17
microteaching laboratories, 14
miseducative, 20
missing link, for reflection, 51
Mitchell, N, 4
Murphy, C, 75, 76
Murray, J, 79
Mutton, T, 20, 79

Napoles, J, 69
Ng, P T, 50
Nicol, D, 66, 68

Office 365 Streaming App, 43, 54

Paivio, A, 30
Paley, V, 31
Palincsar, A S, 75
parallel microteaching, 20
peer feedback, 79
Philipp, R A, 38
Pollard's cycle of reflection, 59
Posner, G J, 76
'The Power of Modeling,' 28
Poyas, Y, 34
pre-packaged prescription, 6
pre-service teachers (PSTs), 1, 3, 20, *see also individual entries*
  benefits of video-based activities, 7
  comments with principles of good feedback, 67–68
  continuous and progressive, experience of reflection, 53
  feedback analyses, 27–28
  feedback on using VideoAnt, 45
  lesson analysis framework, views on, 54
  level of reflection of, 57–58
  quality of reflection, video impact, 56–57
    case study, 57–58
  reflective practice and
    challenges of developing, 49–52
    importance in ITE, 49
    nurturing and promoting within ITE, 51–52
    video-supported model for reflection, 52
  self-efficacy beliefs, 77–78

video analysis tasks for, 36–37
video interaction, 38–41
video recordings, 2–4
acquire, 4
activate, 4
apply, 5
views on microteaching, 22
private curriculum, 33
productive reflection, 56–57
professional vision, 25–26
PSTs, *see* pre-service teachers

recordings, quality of, 2
reflection, 48–49
reflection-in-action, 34
reflective practice, 48–49, 62
challenges of, 52
competing priorities, 50
evidence of its value, 51
limited time and opportunity, 50
reflection format, 50
reflection seem vague and abstract, 49
enhancing quality of, 56–57
and importance in ITE, 49, 51
video-supported model for reflection, 52
nurturing and promoting PSTs, 51
video-supported cycle of reflection, 59
reflective writing, 50
reform-minded teaching, 2
representations of practice, 6–7, 78
Robijns, F, 42, 43
Rogers, C, 49, 56, 58, 61
reflective cycle, 60
Rosaen, C L, 31, 51
Roth, W M, 51
Russ, R S, 26

Sadler, D R, 68
Santagata, R, 30, 69, 79
Scantlebury, K, 75, 76
Scheurman, G, 26
Schön, D A, 13, 49
school experience, 63
learning from, 79–80
SCoTENS, *see* Standing Committee for Teacher Education North and South
SEBs, *see* self-efficacy beliefs
Seidel, T, 60
selective attention, 25
self-efficacy beliefs (SEBs)
in ITE, 77
sources of, 78–79
self-evaluation, annotation for, 44
Sellers, M, 48
Shepel, E L, 77
Sherin, M G, 2, 25, 26, 44
shorter clips, use of, 4
Sigel, I E, 34
Siry, C, 21
Smith, D, 50
Smyth, J, 56
social affordance, of video, 73
Spalding, E, 49
Spiro, R, 6
Standing Committee for Teacher Education North and South (SCoTENS), 15
Stapleton, J, 44
Stein, M K, 9
Stetsenko, A, 73
Stevens, R, 42, 72
Stroupe, D, 5, 73
Studio/Arc, 43
Studiocode software, 44
Swallow, D., 22

Tan, C, 50
teacher educators, 4, 6, 48
teaching, behaviourist view of, 2
technological affordance, of video, 72–73
Tekkumru-Kisa, M, 9
'think-aloud' protocol, 42
Thom, Jamie, 28
time constraints, 50
time-marker, use of, 45
transformative activist stance, 73
Tschannen-Moran, M, 77

van Es, E, 44
VAST, *see* Video Analysis Support Tool
VAT, *see* video analysis of teaching
VELE, *see* video enhanced learning environment
Verbal Persuasion, 79
Vicarious Modelling, 79
video analysis of teaching (VAT), 37
Video Analysis Support Tool (VAST), 44
video annotation, 42
advantages, 43
as interactive viewing guide, 42
for self-evaluation, 44
case study, 44–46
tools, 42–43
VideoAnt, 42, 45, 65
PSTs' feedback on, 45
video-based co-generative dialogue, 21
video-based learning activities, planning of, 9
video conundrum, 8
video enhanced learning environment (VELE), 82
Video in STEM Teacher Assessment (VISTA Project), 15
video interaction, benefits of, 44
video-supported learning activities, 6–7
video-supported model for reflection, 52
case study, 53–56
video-supported zone of proximal development (VSZPD), 75–76
learning to teach, aspects of, 76–77
video technology, 11
video trace, 42

VSZPD, *see* video-supported zone of proximal development
Vygotsky, L S, 73, 74, 76, 77

Ward, J R, 51
Watkins, C, 36
Wilson, A P, 49

Yadav, A, 31
Yerrick, R, 44

Zeichner, K, 13, 20
Zhou, T, 8
zone of proximal development (ZPD), 74–76